Inspirational GOALING

Inspirational GOALING

How Intuition, Passion & a Taste for Adventure Create Goal Victory When Other Methods Haven't

Lynn Moore

Published by Messenger House, Charleston, South Carolina.
Member of Advantage Media Group.

Messenger House is a registered trademark and the Messenger House colophon is a trademark of Advantage Media Group, Inc.

Printed in the United States of America.

ISBN: 978-1-59932-197-4
LCCN: 2010923942

This publication is designed to provide accurate and authoritative information in regard to the subject matter covered. It is sold with the understanding that the publisher is not engaged in rendering legal, accounting, or other professional services. If legal advice or other expert assistance is required, the services of a competent professional person should be sought.

Acknowledgments

Although writing this book seemed like such a lonely endeavor, especially during the long quiet hours of researching, typing, and creative thinking, it really was a team effort. I learned so much about the production of a book and all this entails and if I had not had the amount of hand holding I was given, this book would have forever remained just a dream. Proof that once a solid commitment is made, the Universe sends what and who you need to accomplish that goal.

And so I thank the Divine Source for sending me the idea of traveling to Nepal as a volunteer English teacher to young Buddhist monks and then ever so gently yet persistently poking me until I made a solid commitment.

My gratitude is always and forever extended to everyone I met during my adventures in Nepal: Chris Frazer-Jenkins and the i to i community for arranging my travels and supporting me while there; the hotel staff at the Student Guest House especially Suraj, Suresh and Deepak; all my fellow volunteers notably Charmaine, Rachelle,

Chris (England), Chris (Denmark) and Peter; Dr. Yadav and the staff at Kathmandu Animal Hospital and Research Center; Tenzen Lama and all the Buddhist monks at Sangye Choling Gumpa monastery in Swayambhu; and the Nepali people for their respect and help. I have a high regard and love for you all.

I am forever grateful to Sophfronia Scott and her Business Book Bootcamp writing course which, after my gallant attempt to write my book on my own, not only educated me as to why I quit trying but also went on to give me everything I needed to accomplish this desire I have known all of my life I was meant to achieve. But it didn't stop there. Thanks to Sophfronia's Messenger House Publishing, I found the team at Advantage Media Group, which is filled with so many talented, caring people who took such wonderful care of me and this book. Thank you Denis, Alison, Kim (cover art), Michelle, Scott (editing), and all those behind the scenes whose dedication to authors is refreshing and much appreciated.

Thank you to all my clients, former and current, and friends for their encouragement, praise, and loyalty. You are very special to me.

My gratitude to my family is boundless. To my husband Greg, who has championed me throughout all my endeavors over the years and who has the capacity to love me unconditionally. To our children and grandchildren who have been my magnificent teachers in this school of life by just being who they are, each unique and complete. To my sister Penny, who has been my best friend throughout our lives together, and my 'new' sister, Debbie, who welcomed me with open arms. I deeply love you all.

My everlasting love and gratitude to my parents for their love and dedication to our family and each other. I know they are both looking down with glowing faces full of pride for their first born.

Lastly, thank you Atma, my sweet, wee girl, for placing your life in my hands and rewarding me every day with such devotion, puppy kisses, warm snuggles and our soul connection that sings in my heart with every gaze from your happy, dancing eyes. You changed my life and you inspire me everyday. I love you and will care for you throughout our lives together.

Dedicated to SID

Whose purring was as loud as his snoring, and
whose love for us and ours for him a true soul connection.

I love you, my Beautiful Bengal Boy.

1998–2009

Table of Contents

Introduction

This book is about two journeys: a journey to the Asian old world and a journey to the new world where the 'art of 'Goaling' explores new levels of accomplishment. With the help of a starving, four-footed wee angel who struggles to survive alone in Kathmandu, Nepal, this book will provide insights and epiphanies. In fact, she and I will take you on a journey of enlightenment such as you may never have imagined in its concept and simplicity.

Have you become aware of the shift? In the latter portion of 2008, our world rocked on its economic foundations, and this marked the beginning of making the financial corrections long overdue. However, this 'Shift' is much more than economic. It is a worldwide shift in consciousness—and the news is good! We are coming out of the so-called Information Age and arriving in the Conceptual Age.

This is a fascinating subject about which much is being discussed and written. For people like you and me, we simply want to know how this will affect us when it comes to personal growth, a happy family, nice home, enjoyable career, and feeling confident and happy with our lives.

I didn't know it at the time, but my decision to go to Nepal as a volunteer to teach English to Buddhist monks was my introduction to the Shift a few months before the global economic shift hit. And now as I observe people around me, I see it affecting them, too. We are doing things we never thought we would do. Four of my friends who were dyed-in-the-wool smokers have quit. Three women I know who have been on the heavy side for decades and who swore they were happy that way are now shedding the pounds at Weight Watchers.

We are feeling a need to change instead of fearing change. Spirituality, as opposed to religion, is being talked about much more openly. It used to be that those of us who were spiritual people usually kept it to ourselves, fearing that people would think we were too 'out there'. Now that we are talking about it openly, we are finding out just how many millions of us are on the same path.

This is an incredibly exciting time for all of us. We have begun to make the changes we have wanted to see all our lives. But—good grief—in order for our Divine Source to get our attention, we have to have all our toys taken away. For some, their homes are lost. For others, their jobs disappear. And still more of us, our health goes. We can plop down in a mud puddle and cry our eyes out over our plight, or we can choose to work with the Laws of the Universe (in a later chapter), take ownership of our lives, square our shoulders, and march to a new tempo. One of the ways you can do the latter is to take back your power, steer the ship of your own life, and learn a new and fail-safe goal setting and achievement process that I call 'Goaling,' a process that is synchronized with the energy and in alignment with this planetary Shift.

Speaking of paths, mine had led me to a passion to learn so that I may teach so that I may learn anew. What I teach, Goaling, gives me more than a passing interest in what this Shift is providing in this arena. During the past century, the teaching of goal achievement has been centered predominantly on the left brain, the part of the brain that is linear: that follows steps and sets time limits. That is changing. The whole way of doing business is changing, because the old ways are no longer working. People, especially women, have never wanted to 'be sold' a product, be talked at, or feel pressured. Women prefer 'relationship marketing.' Evidence of this is in the overwhelming number of women in direct or multilevel marketing companies. These businesses have always been built on relationship marketing. Good news for us ladies, as this is part of the Shift, and the success of women in business will rise exponentially. In fact, it is already well on its way. Women naturally know how to market by building relationships with clients.

As women and men, we can begin to dance in tempo with this Shift by incorporating methods using more of the right-brained way of thinking. Rather than predominantly using the left-brained analytical and bullet-pointed 'thinking', we now want to make more use of our creative, free-thinking, heartfelt and soul-directed, intuitive right brain.

Of course, using just the right brain is as silly as using just the left brain, but the secret is to use the whole brain with emphasis on the right. Most of the Goaling methods I teach are right brain oriented, but there is still a need for the talents of the left brain. We need a system of roads and streets and a method of transportation to reach a destination. We are going to use both sides of our brains in this book.

Beautifully blending into this new Conceptual Age is Inspirational Goaling. Briefly and succinctly put, Inspirational Goaling is about thinking in the present moment. Just as the past can be valued only by what we learned from it, the future has only value for what we plan and our ability to be flexible as outside influences demand. We are then left with the present, during which we do have power and control over our lives. Life is a succession of present moments. How do you spend them?

Inspirational Goaling is also about goal *attraction*. Rather than chasing after goals, we can attract them to us like metal to magnets. Remind yourself of the line from the film *Field of Dreams*, "If you build it, they will come." I will teach you what and how to build 'it' so that your goals will come. What are your dreams?

The 'Inspirational' aspect comes in developing a new awareness of your very powerful intuition. Often we are so saturated by our five senses that we forget we have a sixth. Well this sixth sense is sending you text messages every moment of every day with knowledge that is divinely truthful and always guiding you goal ward. Can you 'read' those messages? I will teach you how.

Into all of this will come a dollop of spirituality—the secret ingredient of sorts. Just enough to flavor the pot with that one unidentifiable taste bud treat that causes people to ask, "What is that exquisite taste? What did you put in this? May I have the recipe?" And so I ask you, are your taste buds ready for a treat?

I want you to become aware of a different kind of listening, one that comes from a source of pure love. It takes some work developing new 'ears,' for this source does not speak to any of your five senses. This 'Intuition,' its root word meaning inner teaching, is the teacher inside. You have one, but the din and clatter on this earth drowns it out until you grow your new 'ears,' that is. We will be working on that growth.

Let's take a look at some important topics on which we stumble: seeking, listening, passion, soul connection, and how, in particular, this Shift will have us walking tall and steady.

It seems we are continually seeking, searching for the Holy Grail of happiness, hoping something or someone will have us finally feeling fulfilled, giving us what we want. There are those occasions when we think we have found it at last. "Now I'll be happy," we tell ourselves, only to discover within a short time the feeling of discontent is back, and we find ourselves searching yet again. This happens for a lot of people using the old way of achieving goals.

I have had people tell me that they have tried setting goals but that it never works for them or that they have achieved some goals but their lives still suck. You will find out early in this book that the former is impossible and the latter has a simple solution.

When it comes to being a Seeker, it isn't about looking for answers outside of ourselves, but looking inside for the answers that are already there. How can you know what makes you happy and fulfilled if you don't know who you are? Yes, I know, "Who am I?" tends to be an overworked phrase, and when you think about it, looking in a mirror and asking "Who am I?" when you have spent every waking and sleeping moment of your life with yourself does seem ridiculous.

However, what you see in that mirror is just an ever-changing human form. It is not you. You are an essence, one that has layer upon layer of crud accumulated by your worldly experiences, peer pressure, people-pleasing syndrome, being told how you must be, how you must act, what you must believe and not believe, and so on. If you remember the penny jawbreakers that you popped in your mouth (they could last for twenty minutes if you didn't bite them, and your black tongue and teeth were awesome!), you also remember taking it out of your mouth again and again to see what color the next layer was until you got to that little anise seed in the core. This is what I mean. That precious, miraculous anise seed created by our Source has been smothered in all those layers of dye, artificial flavor, and processed sugar created by us mortals.

We will spend time in this book drilling down through those cruddy layers and finding your 'seed,' your true essence. Without that, your dreams and goals are just what someone or something made you believe would fulfill you. Most reasons for failing to achieve goals are because the goals were not the right ones for you.

Who and what do you listen to? Radio, TV, newspapers, magazines, well-meaning people with harmful messages or even not so well-meaning people are all eager for your eyes and ears. If it isn't for your money for sponsors and advertisers, it is a power they crave. Unfulfilled people need to make others feel unfulfilled, fearful people need to make others feel fearful, victims need to make others feel like victims, and on it goes because it validates where they are in their own lives, and that validation allows them to stay stuck rather than make changes. After all, change (such as quitting destructive habits) might be hard or require working, spending money to take a class, hiring a coach, starting a fitness program, reading a great self-help book and ditching the romance novel, or even setting some goals.

I love to share a funny, tasteful joke, suggest a great book, offer a helpful tip, spend time loving and caring with my pets, enjoying a stimulating conversation, or just savoring quiet time. What I most like to share, though, is knowledge—the greatest motivating factor in writing this book. How about you? What do you share? This becomes center when your goals are defined. It is the big secret to feeling fulfilled, locating the Holy Grail of happiness and living from your Essence. I look forward to working with you in a later chapter on this 'secret.'

I will be sharing with you some personal, often hilarious stories of recent and not so recent adventures along my own path of tenacious seeking, intuitive listening, and passionate sharing of knowledge in order to illustrate to you how they all worked together in one person's life.

A well-known phrase tells us we are not humans having a spiritual experience, but spirits having a human experience – that our souls are not somewhere deep inside our bodies, but our bodies are within our souls. If you know about or have seen an image of someone's aura, then you can then visualize an image of a soul surrounding a body rather than a body enclosing a soul.

We become inspired, meaning 'in spirit,' through our souls. That is why Soul Connection is important. I will be telling you the story of my soul connection with a starving, obviously sick, and mostly hairless four-footed darling who inspired me to walk in a different direction and write this book.

Just as a jumble of jigsaw pieces join together to reveal a beautiful picture, fitting together these pieces of knowledge into your life will remove those layers of crud and expose a clear, stunning vista of your life at its ultimate potential.

An intuitive listener and passionate teacher, bonded together by a taste for adventure and deep desire for a soul connection is indeed someone creating a life of which dreams are made.

Ready to get started?

Chapter One

Those Dang Epiphanies!

Epiphany: The dictionary defines 'epiphany' as a sudden, intuitive leap of understanding, especially through an ordinary but striking occurrence. According to *Lynn's Dictionary*? A shivery, goose-bumpy quiver in your soul.

The moment is forever etched on my memory.

It was a sunny, early summer day. I stood leafing through our Investors Group review magazine expecting nothing but brittle, dry facts and figures on money portfolios and the rising and falling of stocks.

Ho-hum. Yawn.

Had it been a few months later in the year when the world fell into a recession equal to the Great Depression, I may have had more of a panicked interest. But that's beside the point.

Instead, this issue had interesting articles on how we, as citizens of the world, could contribute to the 'greening' of our planet. It seems, along with feeling more responsible and having some form of empowerment over the wastebasket of air, water, and land into which we have turned our world, feelings of philanthropy also sprout in our hearts.

One such example is 'voluntourism,' a method of going on vacation and combining it with volunteering your talents or services in the country you are visiting. Suggestions such as assisting marine biologists in recording the behavior of white sharks in South Africa or building thatched lodges for ecotourists while you discover the ancient civilization of the 'cloud people' in Levanto, Peru, were enticing and tickled my imagination.

There was also a third suggestion. This one did not just tickle. This one sumo-wrestled my imagination into a diaper-wearing, towering dynamo of energy that lasted for all of a split second. It read, "Find your Zen while teaching English to Buddhist monks in the Thamel area of Kathmandu."

Out of my mouth burst the words, "I would love to do that!", Followed by, "Who said that?" as I peered around the vacant room looking for a person other than myself. "That's ludicrous," I thought, "I could never do that." And I put the magazine down.

Too late, the epiphany's arrow had struck home and things were set in motion in my head and heart that I was certain had never moved a millimeter prior to that moment. Things like images of serene, meditation-marinated monks sitting cross-legged on cushions eagerly awaiting the pearls of wisdom only I could share. Or trekking across the top of the world with Everest in sight and lounging in a rickshaw with parasol and carefully packed teaching aids while on my daily commute to the monastery. Perhaps I would leisurely walk the colorful streets of romantic Kathmandu, a city so permeated in ancient history that I could inhale its culture, the sights of exquisite monasteries, the surrounding peaks of snow-capped mountains, and the unique architecture.

Then there were the feelings of such joy and fulfillment that come with planting the seeds of learning and assisting people in their own quests for knowledge and education.

These emotions and scenes kept popping into my head at the most unexpected and inconvenient times. Moments when I was watching American Idol and missed the ever-so-helpful comments of Simon Cowell or after cleaning my eyeglass lenses and being puzzled that my world had become a huge smudge, only to discover I had used hair spray rather than lens cleaner.

As more time passed, it was becoming clear to me that this was not going to leave me alone. For some reason, completely unknown to me, I was supposed to go to Kathmandu and teach English to monks.

The dream book closed and the practicality began when I asked myself, "If I am to do this, how can I make it happen?"

Now, I am pretty good at practical stuff, so this should have been as easy as setting a new goal. Whoa there! A "bingo" moment . . . . That's exactly what I had done! I had just set myself a soul goal and hadn't even thought of it that way. Rather than thinking my way into a target for a goal, the goal found me. I was astounded at this insight.

Had this ever happened to me before?

Now my mind was whizzing back in time faster than film rewinding. What other epiphanies have morphed into goals for me? Let's see . . . .

Before continuing on this expedition, let's take a few steps back and explore your past history of Goaling, what has worked and what has not.

You would likely not be reading this book if you did not want to learn more about goal setting and achieving its mastery. You need to acknowledge something before you can change it, so if you have been disappointed in your past efforts with Goaling, let's go excavating and dig up some of your past experiences.

Let's declare one thing as we begin: the human is hard wired to live by looking to the future.

"And this is his salvation in the most difficult moments of his existence, although he sometimes has to force his mind to the task."
— Viktor Frankl

During difficult, stressful times, inner strength can be had by dreaming of a goal that you can look forward to. Think about this if you have been thrown off balance by the economic Shift. I would add that Viktor Frankl, an eminent psychiatrist, came to his conclusions while spending years mired in the horrors of Nazi prison camps such as Auschwitz and Dachau during World War II.

Frankl also tells us that we can long for times past, and in doing so, we can dream and make the present less painful. But in doing so, we actually make the present pointless. So you can close your eyes, stay in the past, and life in the present will become meaningless, or you can take advantage of the opportunity of difficult times to grow spiritually.

Viktor Frankl's book, *Man's Search for Meaning*, was published in 1946 and still remains a popular book today.

If you are not looking to the future, you are fighting against the grain, swimming against a swift current, climbing mountains with bare feet. Why? **Because you are a goal achiever!** Yes, that is written in stone. It is absolutely true, you can take that to the bank, bet on it, write it in your journal, announce it to the world, put it on a bumper sticker, a T-shirt, a key chain, and your front door. Record it on your iPod, use it as your signature line for all your e-mails, paint it on your toilet seat, stitch it in a sampler, go crazy with the ways you spread your truth!

Go ahead now . . . out loud . . . **"I am a goal achiever."**

Ack! That was terrible. *Out loud*, all the way from your toes: take a deep breath and say it again!

"I AM A GOAL ACHIEVER!"

Much better!

So why don't you feel like one? Ah, there's the catch: How can you be a goal achiever and yet not know how to set goals, be afraid to set goals, or not feel successful in life?

Right now, while you are thinking about it, write down a past experience setting a goal and the outcome.

How do you feel about it now?

Was it a good or not-so-good experience?

What did you learn from it?

____

____

Have you continued to set goals or did you stop after one success or one 'failure'?

____

____

At the end of this book, we are going to return to what you have written here and have you look at it again.

You may feel that life just happens, that you have no control over events that seem to come out of nowhere and leave you with no options other than to react and hope for the best. That's living life on autopilot while someone snoozes at the controls.

If you do not consciously choose and set your goals, then you are unconsciously choosing and setting your goals.

Read that sentence again, out loud.

What I mean by 'going Goaling' is consciously using the power of thought to bring better things to your life.

We will go into that, about the working of your brain, a bit more a little later on. For now, realize that Goaling is all about energies, and you are always vibrating at different energy levels. It is the Universal Law of Attraction (more on these laws later, too) that brings to you what you ask for depending on the intensity of the vibes.

Imagine a stunningly beautiful, bright yellow blossom turning its face to the sunshine and vibrating in sync with the honey bee. The honey bee is on the hunt, crosses paths with the blossom's vibe, and then hones in. A slight hover over the blossom tells the honey bee it has found its target. Quickly and ecstatically, the honey bee slurps up the nectar and at the same time gets its little legs all covered with pollen so that when it buzzes on down the road, it can cross-pollinate to ensure more flowers will bloom. Then it goes home and makes delicious honey. Ingenious!

While the flower is still a bud with its pollen enclosed and developing within, it is not vibrating on the same level; therefore, the honey bee is not yet attracted to the bud. If that flower were a piece of rotting fruit, it would attract flies and not honey bees. It is less pleasing to think of rotting fruit as opposed to bright, yellow blossoms, but nothing in Nature is without a purpose—and that means you, too.

It is a law of nature, just as Goaling is a law of nature.

Take a few minutes and write down some of the things in your life right now that are not to your liking. Don't skip this. (I'm watching you, and I give merit points.)

____

____

____

____

____

____

____

____

____

____

____

So if you are going to be a magnet and attract similar vibrations, they may as well be the ones you have consciously chosen as those you really want. You are a goal achiever, and if you are unhappy with the way life has 'happened,' it is due to thinking thoughts that set up the type of energies that resonate with those thoughts.

If you are continually thinking fearful thoughts of getting sick, guess what? You will get sick, because you are resonating with the energies of illness. If you are continually saying, "I'm having such trouble in history class. I fail all my tests." Guess what? You will continue to have trouble and fail tests.

You can fix this, though. We'll begin with a little exercise.

How do you feel about what I have just explained? Do you feel a bit overwhelmed with the thought that you have this capability and that it is up to you to use it? Do you feel a strong sense of relief knowing that you are empowered and can change your life? However you feel, take a few minutes to write down your feelings. There are no right or wrong answers. Don't hesitate—it's all going to work out great.

____

____

____

____

____

____

____

____

If you are pleased with the way you feel, fantastic! If you aren't, just know that you have acknowledged those feelings and now you have the wherewithal to change them. Just by having the courage to pick up this book, you have demonstrated a desire to change and are already sending out new vibes. Good for you! I'm here as your cheerleader, coach, mentor, teacher, whatever you need me to be, and together we will change your life.

There is another way of looking at the vibration-filled Law of Attraction. It has been my experience that my goals often find me! You don't have to struggle and chase after them. The Law of Attraction does not dangle a chocolate chip cookie just out of your reach. It feeds you the cookie one delicious morsel at a time. The Law of Attraction loves to give; all you have to do is open yourself up and receive.

Think of a time when you have had an epiphany, a truly wonderful thought that entered your brain, did a one-minute tap dance of joy, and then left you tingling with excitement. Do you know what that really is? It is your Divine Source speaking to your soul.

Many times, when these miracles happen, we immediately flip from the soul to the mind only to talk ourselves out of what we just received as a message of direction. We set up detours and roadblocks in the form of excuses and reasons why we cannot follow the directions we just received. Look what I did when I got the message to go halfway around the world and teach English to Buddhist monks! How absurd for me to go so far out of my comfort zone that even the Hubble Telescope couldn't find it. Lucky for me, my guardian angels took up the cause and kept tapping at the door.

There are two more times in my life when a goal found me, both just as profound in result as the most recent excursion to Kathmandu. So here is the rest of the story.

Had this ever happened to me before?

Now my mind is whizzing back through time at the speed of a film rewinding. What other epiphanies have morphed in to goals for me? Let's see . . .

I know! A long time ago, I was in a neighbor's home with a group of other women enjoying a demonstration of skin care products. We were having a hoot of a time cream smearing, mud packing, and scent smelling all between sips of wine and munching on goodies provided by the hostess. In fact, I was so happily engrossed in the event, I almost didn't pay attention to a whisper in the back of my brain saying, "You could do these demonstrations, you know."

But I did hear it, and my instant reaction was, with a derisive snort, "Don't be an idiot!" Once again, it was too late. The seed had been stamped into fertile soil. The thought kept coming back. Ding! Round one, ding! Round two, ding, ding, ding—until I finally accepted that for some reason, I was meant to do this and had to find a way to make it happen.

Happen it did. For the next 20 years, I grew an organization within the company and earned a wonderful income, four new cars, magical trips to destinations around the world for my husband and me, and recognition by the shipload.

Yep, the goal found me.

Oh, and here's a more recent one. Two years ago, during a challenging time, my hubby said to me, "Sometimes I feel like just running away."

To which I empathetically replied, "I think I'd go with you!"

We had a giggle about it and went about our day. This time, though, it wasn't words that came to me but rather a deep, resonating chord of music, something like you would hear from a handcrafted cello played by a master. The rich reverberations bounced from cell to cell within my body until a few days later, they actually formed words: You could if you sold your house.

"What!? Sell our home that we just fully repainted and decorated and in which we planned to spend the rest of our lives? No way."

Sheesh, here we go again. The brain would not shut up. Images of immediate retirement choices were fast-forwarding (there's that film again) through my mind, with a growing sense of freedom swelling to such a size that I had to share it with my hubby or I might explode.

"We could 'run away' if we sold the house," I blurted.

Silence.

A quizzical expression formed on his face.

"Could you really do that?" he asked.

Growing more convinced every second, I answered, "You know, I think I could."

Three months later found us living very comfortably in a 43-foot, late model RV at home on our new deeded property in a lovely RV resort with a western boundary that kisses a lakeshore and an eastern boundary with hills that stretch to the sunrise every morning. It may be only an RV pad, but dang, living on lakeshore property had never entered our minds!

We have now spent the past three winters in southern Arizona, where the Canadian winters are nothing more than an icy memory. Making new friends, reconnecting with old friends, speeding along the highways on our motorcycle, and economizing while leaving less of a carbon footprint by scooting about in our Smart Car are just some ways we bring joy in to our lives.

And again, the goal found us.

There are more examples of goals finding me throughout my life, but I think you have the picture with these three foundation-shaking, sudden right-turn events. Enough so that you might think that I would have understood long before teaching English to Buddhist monks in Nepal that something was going on here, something that I should be paying attention to, something that I should be sharing with other human beings.

Well, some of us have to be tapped, some of us have to be slapped, and some of us need to be walloped on the head. I got walloped on the head and learned that the best goals were the ones that found me. Later on, I was taught the next step – yes, there is more – through the soulful eyes and strong heart of a wiggly, four-footed friend.

Resources

Man's Search For Meaning, Viktor Frankl

TUT's Adventure Club, http://www.tut.com/?a_aid=goaling
The amazing Mike Dooley offers his "Notes From the Universe" five days a week with free registration. Funny, whimsical, and right on the button, this is the only daily message subscription that I have never cancelled. For three years, I have been receiving my 'note,' without reruns, and it never fails to be a daily highlight.

Chapter Two

Connecting with Purpose

Travel: The dictionary defines 'travel' as a journey to an unfamiliar place, usually using a form of transportation. *Lynn's Dictionary* defines travel as 'a sport of Olympic proportions, involving Herculean endurance while hurtling through time zones and space in a yo-yo-like fashion while squished into a stamp-sized seat inside a metal tube.'

Eleven months post-epiphany.

Teaching English as a Foreign Language course completed. ✔
All vaccinations completed. ✔
Nepali visa taken care of. ✔
Indian visa (don't even ask why it was needed!) in passport. ✔

Flights booked and confirmed. ✔
Medical insurance purchased. ✔
Passport, plane tickets, bank card, Visa card, and a small amount of U.S. cash velcroed to my body. ✔
Luggage packed. ✔
Hubby waiting in car while I have a last kitty cuddle (sniff, sniff). ✔

It's time for lift-off.

Anyone who has traveled by air recently knows the size and weight restrictions for baggage are becoming as difficult to decipher as tax forms. Not to mention that if the rules become any more restrictive, we will soon have to choose between taking a toothbrush or a change of undies in a brown paper bag. We will have to be ten pounds less than our ideal body weights, and the food served on board will be puffed pork rinds, and all this after a fuel surcharge equal to the cost of a royal wedding.

Now, I do have a reason for my slightly caustic tongue on this subject. I have a practical nature, and it seems to me, due to the fact that one of my two pieces of luggage (I'm allowed two only because I'm flying halfway around the world) was pretty much empty (in anticipation of the vast amounts of treasure I would bring home), I could put one suitcase inside the other, thus allowing both baggage handlers and myself only to deal with one bag. Brilliant!

Checking in now. The lovely lady at the counter says, "I'm sorry, Ms. Moore, but your luggage is overweight. Would you like to pay the overweight fee or remove some of your belongings?" The bag was 'overweight' by all of two pounds. I try to appeal to her sense of reason by pointing out that my body weighs less than the average prepubescent child and that should make up for the overage. I get a look that I translate as, "Would you like to join your luggage in the cargo compartment?"

The result? I'm now down on the floor, both suitcases wide open with my personals on display, transferring a carefully chosen selection (read, taking an armful and dumping) from the loaded suitcase into the empty one. Here's the deal. One suitcase cannot weigh more than 70 lbs, but two can weigh 40 lbs each. Huh? I'll let you figure it out.

Back to check-in counter. I now have two pieces of luggage, both weighing well under the limit, and this entails waiting for two pieces at the luggage carousels, wrestling two pieces onto a cart, and opportunities for two pieces to get lost. Double your pleasure, double your fun!

The first leg is from Kelowna to Calgary: a short, uneventful hop.

The second leg is an Air Canada flight from Calgary to Frankfurt. Why is it that we peons have to trek through first class on our way to the general population section? And it's one of those new first-class sections, with sleeping pods, privacy, and no need to wait to go potty until your snoozing seatmates awaken so you can roust them out of their comfort zones and into the aisles.

Oops. There's a cart in the way.

Oh.

They're bringing alcohol. I'll wait.

I sling back my gin and tonic. Now, the coast is clear. Dang! The tabletops are down. My seatmates are sipping! Don't they know how to sling a drink? An agonizing 20-minute seat-dance later and here comes the cart to collect garbage.

No!

"Would you care for another drink, ma'am?" I hear. Oh sure, why not stretch my bladder all the way to the cockpit?

Thankfully, my seatmates also turn down the offer, garbage is removed, tabletops are placed in the upright position, and I politely ask my partners to excuse me please.

Whew, now I'm upright and in the aisle and turn to sedately make my way down the 'mile aisle' towards the back of the aircraft . . . erch! The flight attendant is now an eyelash away from my face, calmly and socially continuing to offer and serve drinks at the speed of melting ice.

Finally! The lavatory door is right in front of me. As I stare open-jawed and confused by the 'occupied' on the door, my brain formulates the words, "How did it become occupied when no one could get past the cart?"

Oh.

There are two aisles on this plane, and the other one was free of any carts.

After what I am sure was the reading of 'War and Peace', a fellow passenger exits the lavatory. At last, it is all mine!

Tucked back in my seat, I pass the next several hours staring at a marathon of movies I selected on the screen in the seatback in front of me. Marvelous invention!

I decide to try for some shut-eye. But it's not happening.

Some kind of meal was tossed on my tray from the now rapidly moving cart. Don't eat the red sauce. I recognized fruit salad and a bun. They're safe.

Some time later, I deplane in Frankfurt and follow the signs to my next departure gate on Lufthansa to New Delhi. I follow the signs, follow the signs, and follow the signs until it becomes evident I must be walking to New Delhi!

There's my gate, Z-one-thousand or so. I sit and stare at a German newspaper until the flight is called and the cattle stampede begins.

What's different about Lufthansa?

Well, I have a stainless steel fork with which to eat more fantasia food. No broken plastic prongs as this fork is forced through Jell-O. It's back to the TV hanging from the ceiling, and I already saw the movie. Might as well have another G&T.

No miniature bottle of gin this time either. They must have Fritz the bartender in back shaking, stirring, and mixing for us. The first sip hollers at me that the ratio of 'G' is far greater than 'T.' I manage a gasp of air as the spasms in my swallowing mechanism relax. It's no surprise I'm finally able to catch a nap.

Our destination is New Delhi, so I notice we have a good number of Indian passengers, among them several children. I find myself jolted from my short nap by the screech of attempted High Cs by the Delhi Boys Choir, seemingly hit all at the same time. The performance went on for the duration of the flight which was a sleepless and interminable six hours.

Landing and deplaning in Delhi, I try not to shoot visual daggers at the angelic faces of the guilty and instead aim a little higher at the faces of their indulgent parents. It's after midnight; I have to collect my baggage (I never got a satisfactory answer as to why my baggage couldn't be forwarded to Kathmandu), wrestle it onto a luggage cart, and spend the next six hours sitting in a somewhat wider but still uncomfortable seat or wandering the airport while pushing my cart. The check-in counter for the next flight will not be open until one hour before the flight; therefore, I spend the hours developing a great respect for bag ladies.

I have a dilemma. How does one get a luggage cart into the bathroom where the door is narrower than the loaded cart? I'm thinking a catheter for my next long trip will solve many problems. That and some knock-out pills—for the Delhi Boys Choir, not me. After more pacing and especially after learning that the next flight will be an hour delayed, I realize I'm going to have to reach out and trust somebody to watch my luggage while I get in-and-out of the bathroom in record time. I found an English-speaking woman happy to help, and since then I have written my letter to the Guinness Book of World Records.

After what seems the longest night of my life, I'm finally at the check-in counter for Jet Airways, which is going to take me on the final leg of my journey to Kathmandu. I smile at the woman behind the counter and gratefully hand over my bags. My smile morphs into a jaw drop when she says, "You are only allowed one piece of baggage. You will have to pay extra." Here I go again, dealing with another official suffering from baggage-itis. I explain, with as much clarity as a foggy day, that I have come from Canada to spend six weeks in Nepal and that a one-piece limit is unreasonable and bordering on stupid.

I get resistance, and I respond with more jet-lagged gibberish until she finally consults one of her cohorts, shows her my complete flight itinerary, and with a shrug and a muttered tells me, "Here's your boarding pass." She waves me through. I stagger to security with an "I won" feeling holding me upright.

The flight to Kathmandu is a blessed 70 minutes. We land in a torrential downpour, the first rain the city has had for months. So much rain, in fact, that my soft-sided luggage is unable to keep the wetness from infiltrating my belongings during the short trip from the aircraft to the terminal.

After a person in a white coat and face mask gives us a form to complete and asks if we have had a cold, sore throat, cough, or flu-like symptoms recently (this method is supposedly going to keep the H1N1 flu out of Nepal), we fill in the form and return it to the medical personnel. I ask you, is anyone going to answer yes to any of those questions? Not when the alternative might be getting back on a plane.

Then, there's a stampede to a desk with visa forms everyone must fill out. This is a second visa form. For some reason as a volunteer, I have to have two forms. I search for 15 minutes for one in English, attempting to push my short arms between people crushed together. I finally find one on the floor, stamped with a shoeprint.

Now I'm at the end of the immigration line. Eventually, I reach the desk, pay for my visa, show my passport, and get asked for a passport-size photograph to staple to my visa. I know I put it in a convenient place where I could retrieve it in two seconds. Everyone else is gone, but I'm left muttering and digging in my carry-on bag with no photo to be found. So befuddled, exhausted, and dizzy-headed by now, I put my head on the counter and fought sleep.

I was roused a few minutes later by an official holding up my passport and asking, "Is this you?" I nod yes and am told I can go through. In the baggage claim area, there is not a single person and just two bags on the floor . . . mine. Finding a rusted, lumpy-wheeled cart, I once again load up my bags and head out the door to be met by my volunteer coordinator in Nepal.

He is not there.

I am stranded in a foreign country, can't speak the language, and only have my familiar baggage for company.

The journey to your goal's accomplishment will be filled with tests. They are necessary, for it is the journey that determines how valuable the goal's achievement will be. Much as we would like to believe it, rubbing a lamp to make a genie appear and instantly receiving our wishes would never be fulfilling. That would be far too easy, and we humans just don't put much value on easy or free things.

So what will carry us through these times of testing? Do you think I wanted to turn around and book a flight back home right to my comfort zone? You betcha! That comfort zone was standing with open arms and beckoning me, and I desperately wanted to climb right into that zone and curl into a ball. My goal, however, was connected to something—something very powerful and strong. It was connected to something that was whispered in my ear at the time I drew my first breath.

The messenger doing the whispering was my Guardian Angel, sent by the Divine Source. After giving me my message, she placed her finger perpendicularly over my lips, directly under my nose, and whispered, "Shhh." Meaning my purpose was now in me, and my duty was to discover it. The angel left an imprint on my face, and that is why we all have a small dip in the space between the center of our upper lip and our nose. Ever notice how we place our forefinger there when we are deep in thought? Go ahead, place your finger on it right now and very gently feel it as you imagine your own Guardian Angel delivering your purpose to you. Magical, isn't it?

That purpose is driven by a passion so strong that it will drive us, support us, and carry us over, under, and around whatever obstacles stand in our way. It provides us with courage and stamina through which nothing can penetrate to cause us to deviate from our path.

I know my purpose and passion. They stood, one on either side of me, offering their strength and support that day I arrived in Kathmandu, Nepal, when I found myself alone and stranded.

Even if you have no words to describe what it is that keeps you strong when in the face of adversity, you have 'that thing,' and it is there. If you think back to a time in your life when you felt like a champion, beginning when you were just a little child, you can begin to feel it again. Children naturally act out their 'purposes' purely from the right brain. It's only as we become adults with the buildup of the cruddy layers of influence that this becomes more difficult.

You are about to embark on a series of exercises. Before you do this, I want us to take a moment so I can share something with you. Life is a series of 'now' moments. Your past, that is your history, only has power as a fountain of invaluable experiences from which you can drink. Your future is for planning. It will always be a mystery until it becomes a 'now' moment. But as we already know, we are programmed to think towards the future, and in doing so, we find hope and motivation to create and plan. Your 'now,' that is your present, is for choosing and doing.

You recently had a 'now' moment when you made a choice and picked up this book. Something about it told you it might have something to do with planning a better future for you. And you were right.

As you continue through this book, I want you to appreciate that life really is a series of 'now' moments for choosing and doing. These exercises are planned precisely to lead you to a transformed future. If you don't wish to do the exercises in the 'now' moments in which they are presented to you, I would rather you put this book down and return to it when you are ready to work in the 'now.'

Reading this book all the way through first and then coming back to the exercises to do them won't work when it comes to my method of Goaling. It is an unfolding process of awareness and action, awareness and action. Learning how to use your 'now' moments leads to authentic inner change, which means you have command of your own destiny.

With this in mind, take some time now and think back. This exercise is one wherein your past assumes its role as teacher. Think as far back as your memory can stretch and begin to write down those times when you felt courageous, strong, accomplished, bright, joyous, or any other 'winning' feelings.

____

____

____

____

____

____

____

____

____

____

____

____

____

____

____

____

This is not something we often give ourselves the pleasure to think about, and at first it might seem difficult. But I promise you, once the door is opened and you write the first two or three champion experiences, the flow will begin and the memories will start to stream from your consciousness and on to the paper. In fact, you may need to add another piece of paper. So go ahead – make yourself happy!

Now you have your foundation: the beginning of discovering what it is that you were put on this earth to do. Once you have the words to define what that is, you will have revealed the secret to your existence. Things will make sense that once didn't. You will have a sense of direction where once you felt lost. You will be anchored rather than drifting. A sense of purpose carries you home to your desires, home to your contribution, and home to a joy and happiness that will uplift you as long as you are here.

It makes me think of George, played by Jimmy Stewart in *It's a Wonderful Life*, as he runs down the snow-covered street of his town shouting in happiness, slipping and sliding and laughing on his way home to his family on Christmas Eve after receiving his 'gift' from his own Guardian Angel, Clarence.

Step One

Let's begin the search for some of the words you need to best express your purpose.

From your 'champion' list above, choose one of those times when you felt like a champion. Begin with, "I remember the time when I ________." Tell the story of that time and how you felt in two to three paragraphs.

Don't jump ahead. Stop at this point and do this exercise. This is very important. I'm happy to wait.

(Imagine the song 'Feelings' playing for as long as you need.)

Done?

Very good! I'm proud of you.

Repeat this step for two more stories taken from your list.

(More music.)

Now, read over your stories. Without thinking, just feeling, circle the words you have written that strike some kind of chord with you. Maybe you see that you have used the same word several times in all the three stories. This is a clue that it's an important word to you. Listen to your heart as you read your stories, feel the swell in your chest, the blush in your cheeks, and the small smile that tugs at the edges of your lips. These are your emotions those words cause. And because our right brain thinks in pictures, it is these words that draw the pictures that you want.

Now, make a list of your important words.

____

____

____

____

____

____

____

____

____

____

____

____

____

____

____

The time has come to test the words. Ask a trusted person, someone close to you, to speak the words one at a time in random order. When you hear the word, pay close attention to what that word evoked in you emotionally the instant you heard it. Maybe there was a mild reaction, no reaction, a neutral reaction, or a heart string was plucked and you may have even had a physical reaction. Your trusted person should watch you for these and comment. If no chord is struck, eliminate that word.

Now, you'll need to share the following note with your trusted person: Your role here, a place of honor, is to support your friend in this important exercise. You are bearing witness to a very exciting unveiling. It is best if you refrain from suggesting words or making comments other than as described above. Any hint of judgment on your part can throw this exercise off course and may even halt your friend's progress. Bless you for accepting this undertaking and helping your friend discover their purpose in this lifetime.

Your list of words should now have been refined. You will usually have a mixture of nouns, verbs, adjectives, and adverbs, and now it is time to play with them.

The role of the trusted person is to remain neutral and not pass judgment, as this is your purpose and no one can tell you what it is or how to word it. It is completely based on you and your feelings, so keep out any analyses! This is a heart exercise, and emotions spring from the heart. You will need a pad of paper to try several combinations of your words to form one sentence, and that will be the description of your purpose. This is a very exciting time, and I want you to feel that excitement!

This is your start:

I am a ________________ woman/man ____________________

....

...."

Use a descriptive word in the first blank that tells what kind of person you are, e.g., gentle, strong, imaginative, lighthearted, joyous. You will find this word in your list.

Follow that with an action word in the second blank that describes what you do, e.g., love, dance, care, help, forgive.

Remember, these words are taken from your list of important words.

Keep the words in the present tense. Don't use actions from the past or words ending in *-ed*, e.g., help and not helped, seek and not sought, pray and not prayed. Also, don't put your words in the future tense, e.g., help and not will be helping, seek and not will seek, pray and not will pray.

Now go for it! You and your partner write and rearrange. Try a sentence out loud, reverse words, add *-ing* to one just to play with it. Don't over analyze, and keep your feelings in the forefront. It may come quickly or take 5 to 10 minutes. That's all.

You will know when it comes together. Some people laugh, some are moved to tears, some jump up in the air, and some smile widely and their eyes dance. You *will* feel it!

I will divulge my own purpose right here in its entirety so you can see how a purpose sentence appears:

I am a strong woman leading people to discover their true value.

When I read it, type it, or say it I feel a swelling in my chest, a smile on my face, and a feeling of 'Yes, that's me!" and I have been feeling that for the past 13 years.

What did you notice about my purpose sentence? Every purpose sentence that has true power includes this. Take a moment to think before continuing.

If you discovered that my purpose involved giving in some way, you are right. I am a leader, and for me, what better way to lead than to help people discover themselves and how valuable they are to themselves and others on this earth.

You can't give without receiving. It's a Universal Law.

You may be an artistic person and able to draw your purpose. I'm one of those who can't even draw a recognizable stick man! But if you have the gift, I urge you to draw or paint a picture of yourself expressing your purpose. Maybe you have a photograph of yourself involved in an activity that communicates how you live your purpose.

And then there is music. Do you play an instrument? Or is there a piece of music that you just love and seems to touch your soul every time you hear it? Listen to that music and allow your feelings to swell as you imagine yourself doing things you love. If you write music, you could compose a piece that comes from your soul and brings to light the message that you are here to deliver.

Step Two

Behind every purpose, there is passion. This is what you are feeling when your purpose sentence is used. Your passion is *how you express your purpose*. What do you love to do? What were you good at in school, your best subject? What kinds of employment have you had that you most enjoyed?

Expression can be done so many ways using the whole body. The mind is used by creating written words, pieces of art, public speaking or teaching; the body can be engaged with dance, sports, modeling, cooking, or landscaping; and the soul can be expressed in spiritual meditations, prayer, or intuitive gifts. These are just a few examples. Notice that all of them involve creating (right brain).

Of course, we use our minds when we pray, our bodies when we give a speech, and our souls when we dance, but one of these (the mind, body, and soul) will become the focal point of expression in each.

The definition of your passion is general and not specific to how you indulge in your passion, e.g., "My passion is preparing nutritious food so that people can improve their health and enjoy life," and not, "My passion is working at Garden Creations Natural Restaurant feeding people healthy food." See the difference?

I will share my passion with you so that you can see how it flows from my purpose.

My passion is to learn so that I may teach so that I may learn anew.

A great clue for me is that my favorite store is a bookstore! I always have my nose in a book or in a computer, and I am always attracted to ways in which I can learn in order to pass it on. I never wanted to just learn something for my own gain alone. There has always been this need for me to share it with others—hopefully to help them some way.

What is your favorite store? And why is it your favorite? These can be your clues to help you find your passion.

How have I expressed my passion to first learn, then teach, and then learn again in my life? Well, I had a business selling a natural, botanically sourced skin care line of product (the first of its kind) about which I was very passionate for 20 years. By teaching people how, when, and why to use it and the benefits they would receive, I fulfilled my purpose and passion. And this is what made my career successful. (My first job, at the age of 15, was as a clerk in a candy store, and I was passionate about candy!)

People purchased the product, used it correctly and in the proper amounts twice daily. They knew the importance and safety of the natural ingredients, and within a short time, they saw in their glowing skin the health benefits of doing what I had taught them. Their testimonials and their gratitude were music to my soul; I was fulfilling my purpose with my passion.

Next, I switched my business emphasis to treatments for the skin, helping people improve their health and appearance even more. While doing this, I taught them how and why they could change or improve other aspects of their daily lives to build upon what I had originally helped them achieve. Often, we start with our outside appearance to help us feel better about something going on inside. I wanted to help people with their overall health: physical, mental, and emotional. This then led to my current career as a life coach.

Look at your history. What have you done with hobbies, careers, and so on? How do they tie in with your purpose and passion? Or how do they not tie in? I recall working as an office assistant, and that certainly did not tie in. I didn't enjoy it and, therefore, it didn't last very long. I had the whole department figured out in a month and made suggestions as to better efficiency and effectiveness. Why it fell on deaf ears and the hierarchy didn't appreciate it was a total puzzle to me! I could never be 'the girl in her cubicle,' head down at her computer (typewriter at the time), and a quiet little mouse in the corner. Anyone who knows me will get a great kick out of that visual!

Now let's gather your clues together.

As a child, I was good at____________________________________

____.

My best classes in school were_______________________________

____.

The job I most enjoyed was__________________________________

____.

My favorite store is_______________________________________

____.

Remembering that your passion is how you express your purpose. Form a sentence that does this for you.

____

____

____

____

So now you have your purpose and your passion defined. You should be feeling really good about this!

The final step, and the easiest one, is your mission.

Your Purpose is your *what*, your Passion is your *why*, and your Mission is your *how*.

How do you use your life to express your passion? If we look back at our example of our cook, whose passion is preparing nutritious food, he uses his passion by working in Garden Creations Natural Restaurant. This is how his purpose and passion are put to use.

You can see in my own example that my passions were used in the sales and service industries, selling a specific product, and later performing specific treatments. And the most recent method, the one I am so enthusiastic and over the moon about, is my career as a life coach.

My mission in my business, Clear Goals Coaching, is to encourage people to accomplish their goals by providing them with specific tools, guidance, and knowledge to help them lead lives of greater fulfillment and abundance. I am in business to fill the need for people to feel optimistic and empowered.

So let's recap:

- **Your Purpose**: Who you are and what you are on this earth to do for others
- **Your Passion:** Why you love to live your purpose and the drive behind your purpose
- **Your Mission:** How you live in concert with your purpose and passion

Our nutritious chef may have a purpose, passion, and mission something like this:

"I am a kind man creating ways for people to enjoy excellent health. My passion is preparing nutritious food so that people can enrich their lives through good food. And my mission is to build an exciting, nutritious menu at Gardens Creations Natural Restaurant to encourage people to visit regularly and learn to enhance their eating habits and love a healthy lifestyle."

As you can expect, one's mission will flex perhaps as one moves from one career to another, but the foundation and the spirit remain the same.

My experience in Nepal was based on my purpose, my passion, and the spirit of my foundation. This is what held me to my mission of teaching English to Buddhist monks rather than entertaining ideas of going home when I was exhausted after four flights, 36 hours of travel, and seemingly abandoned in a world unlike anything I had ever known.

Your Purpose, Passion, and Mission are your three Guardian Angels who are with you throughout your life.

Chapter 3

Shock Value

Shock: The dictionary defines 'shock' as an unexpected, intense, and distressing experience that has a sudden and powerful effect on somebody's emotions or physical reactions. *Lynn's Dictionary* defines 'shock' as discovering not everyone speaks English!

I have officially arrived in Nepal.

An essential part of accomplishing my goal is done. All the action steps I call Mini Goals that lead up to the realization of the Big One. Mini Goal number one was to get to Nepal. Accomplished!

Now I am faced with a challenge, and we will see of what I am made.

The good news? I have all my luggage. I don't take that for granted anymore, I see it as bloody good luck. It's all I can do to not pump my fist and holler an emphatic "Yes!" when I see my bag come down the chute these days.

The not so good news? My contact person, Chris Fraser-Jenkins, is nowhere to be seen. I am standing outside the airport with my cart facing a phalanx of Nepali taxi drivers with dollar signs rolling in their eyes like Las Vegas slot machines.

I am not unprepared for just such an eventuality. I have phone numbers, but I have no phone. Looking around, I see no public phones. I will eventually learn there are few in Kathmandu but virtually everyone has a cell phone. So, I don't have a choice; I must face the barrage of taxi drivers.

I eyeball the taxi driver nearest me and am flummoxed to hear him speak something resembling English. I ask him if he perhaps has seen a gentleman about the age of 60 waiting with an "i to i" sign. He tells me that he did but that he left.

"Where you go? I take you," he says.

"I'm supposed to phone Chris if he is not here," I say as I rummage through my carry-on bag, which seems to have already eaten my passport photo and which I'm hoping didn't make a dessert out of my emergency contacts page. Whew, found it.

My new-found friend asks me for the number and tells me he will use his cell phone to make the call. Seems Chris FJ is known around the airport as he is there picking up volunteers for i to i on a fairly frequent basis. The number is dialed and I hear the taxi driver say "Hello . . . ? Hello . . . ? Hello?" This is when I learn that cell phone service in Kathmandu is about as reliable as a politician's promise. We try several more times and at last reach a voice at the other end. He hands me the phone, and I try mightily to make myself understood by the woman with whom I am speaking. We eventually understand enough of each other's Pidgin English to the point where it seems Chris does not have his cell phone with him, and I should take a taxi to the hotel.

At this point, four more 'helpers' surround me, all chatting in Nepali with each other with an English word tossed in occasionally. I ask the general assembly, "Does anyone know where the Student Guesthouse is?" A chorus of yeses resounds in response. I have yet to learn that a Nepali taxi driver will answer yes to any question regarding where a place is in Kathmandu, and upon not being able to find it, he will flag down one of his cohorts (taxis busily crawl the city like ants on an ant hill) for a conference. Other drivers not currently engaged with a fare also join in, and there is much chattering, arm pointing, and discussing until your driver pops back in the car to resume your journey.

My friend with a phone says he has a vehicle large enough for me and my luggage, and one of his buddies runs off to get it while he wheels my cart for me in the direction of a street. We meet up, my luggage is loaded inside the oddest, most dilapidated van-type thing on wheels, and the driver's buddy hops in the passenger seat, then the driver boards and turns to me in the back and says, "Twenty dollars U.S., OK?" Well, what do I know? Seems pretty reasonable to me.

Speaking of $20, when the general assembly learned I was Canadian, one of the assembled drivers approaches me with a fist full of Loonies and Toonies (Canadian vernacular for one and two dollar coins) and asks me if I could give him $20 U.S. in exchange for them. I guess the banks in Nepal don't take exchange coins, and he must have received them as tips from other Canadians. I made the switch for him.

Now that it appears I am on my way to my hotel, I suddenly realize I have been inhaling a peculiar odor since I exited the airport. I am never able to identify it, but before I leave this country, I simply name it the Kathmandu odor soup. Not pleasant.

Here is when the shock assault begins. I lost count of the number of times my head hit the ceiling of the 'van.' A rougher ride would have to be on a one-humped camel in full gallop (do camels gallop?). The 'streets' are part pothole, part broken pavement, part dirt, narrow and crowded with taxis, rickshaws, pedestrians, stray dogs, motorcycles, buses, and bicycles. It's not traffic, it's a competition! My driver plays what seems an impromptu adaptation of The Ride of The Valkyries on his horn masterfully yet continuously. Other drivers add to the cacophony with their own horn-based melodies.

What I see is difficult for my brain to compute. Dirt and dust are everywhere. Buildings are very old and appear filthy, while stinking smoke from burning mystery piles assaults my eyes and nose. It is beastly hot, and I begin a six-week sweat that never lets up.

At this juncture, my brain forms the words, "Whose insane idea was this?" I tell you now, that once ensconced upon your goal journey, you will have times when you question your sanity. It's normal. But at the time, panic is the only feeling of the moment. Just remember to trust and to have faith.

The driver and his buddy in the front are gesticulating and chattering directions to each other until the taxi comes to a stop in the middle of the street and both escorts exit the vehicle and disappear. Where are they? Where am I? Am I abandoned? I'm thinking, here I am in a foreign country, in a huge city, and have just handed over my safety to two strange men, got in their vehicle, and am now at their mercy. Idiot!

As more minutes pass, my sweating increases with the stress of wondering what I am supposed to do. Just sit here? Follow them? Get out and stand around? And I'm now beginning to hear things—must be the heat—I think I am hearing an English voice. The voice is followed by a body which reaches out and slides open the van door. The voice greets me by name, and I am finally face to face with Chris FJ. In my exhaustion, I want to weep with relief, throw my arms around his waist, and sob, "Daddy, where were you, I was lost!" The small child within is always a part of us.

Chris FJ makes a very quick and assertive change to the $20 fare I have been charged for my introductory tour of Kathmandu. He pays the driver in Nepali rupees, which I later learn is Rs. 250, the usual rate (about $4 CA!). Yeah, I'm sure I saw sucker written across my forehead the next time I peered into a mirror.

Between Chris FJ and me, we wrestle my luggage up three flights of stairs to my room. Why not take an elevator, you ask? Not wise in a country where the electricity fails several times per day, the average amount of availability is only 8 hours out of 24. The sound of noisy old generators (fuel-operated) raises the decibel level of the city during those times.

In my room, Chris FJ makes me aware of a few important facts, such as it may take 4 to 5 minutes for hot water to reach the third floor, so let it run and be patient. I can take my laundry to the desk at any time, and I will pay a certain amount per kilo to have it done. Never, never drink tap water. A medical shop is right across the street where I can get everything from antibiotics to Band-Aids to medical advice from the attendant as to what my needs are. I'm told not to give money to the street kids or the mothers with babies who beg for milk. Sounds cruel, but when you learn why later on in this book, you will understand. No country, it seems, is beyond corruption.

When I want the room cleaned, I simply ask at the desk. I may have to ask several times before it is actually done, but just start asking several days before you really want action. I have a ceiling fan! I'm giving thanks on my knees because my sweat glands have been at full capacity, and I will discover that they won't turn off until I leave the country. I also have artificial light in the form of a single, bare bulb. The bulb and I become great buddies over the next six weeks. It's not her fault she won't function when electricity can't turn her on.

The bathroom is really fun. A western toilet (again, I'm on my knees), a sink, and . . . where is the tub? Shower? I look up. There is a shower head and taps on the wall. Apparently the entire room is the shower enclosure. I eventually find it very efficient in that the whole room gets cleaned as I do. Tiles on walls and floor make for waterproofing, but it's a good idea to keep the toilet lid down, or else the seat gets soaked and the following sit-down can be a bit slippery with all kinds of accompanying gestures, yelps, and bodily adjustments. Oh yes, I also have a bare bulb high up out of the reach of shower spray.

As Chris FJ exits, I race to turn the ceiling fan on full blast and stand under it, gulping the moving air. Next, a shower. I wait the required 4 to 5 minutes and, sure enough, I get semi-hot water. I know that dinner for i to i volunteers is at 7:00 p.m., and it's now about 2:30 p.m. I unpack and, in spite of roaring jet lag and running on fumes, I do a decent job of placing my belongings in a rather neat and effective order. I really want to make it to 7:00 p.m. to meet some of my colleagues.

At 3:00 p.m., I am horizontal on a surprisingly comfortable bed. And I fall unconscious for the next 16 hours.

"The truth of a person is in their behavior, not in their word."
— Sylvia Browne

Whether we are conscious of it or not, we live our lives according to what we value. I'm speaking of intangible values, such as honesty, freedom, independence, and not the tangible things we value, such as a type of house, certain clothing, and fresh cut flowers on the dining table. Not that we don't deserve the comforts of a home, dressing to our liking, or admiring the beauty of flowers. These are important too, but these are external examples of more deep-seated intangible values.

Having a value of 'family happiness' could be the driving force for a type of home that is roomy, ranch-style, or in the country, whatever contributes to the happiness of your family. A style or type of clothing may be an expression of your value of 'self-respect,' and fresh flowers in your home may demonstrate your value of 'beauty.'

I would love to have fresh flowers delivered weekly to my home. And I would, except my dang cats would eat them! I value having my cats more than having flowers in my home, so that's a no-brainer.

One of my values is commitment. I admire dependability in others and have a strong need to remain committed to my word. What do you think kept me anchored to my goal in Nepal when every sense in my body was screaming, "What have you done? The noise, the smells, the dirt, the crowding, the heat, the humidity – how can you live in this for six weeks?" Of course, it was my strong sense of commitment that would not allow me to quit and told me that I would be just fine, just give it some time.

It is your values that also help carry you past any stumbling blocks on the journey to your goal fruition. Therefore, your goals need to be aligned with your values just as much as they are with your purpose and passion. Without that, it would be as if you had an ignition key in a car without gas. As an example, if you have a 'you-should' goal (the kind that someone in authority strongly suggested) to rent a home with five friends in order to keep costs down, but one of your values is peace, either the goal will not come about or it will, and you will be most unhappy and inclined to declare that goals don't work for you.

Before you take a close look at what you truly value, let's examine what a value is and is not.

Let's be clear that your values are not what you think you should be, they are who you are right now. Who you are is identical to what you value. How you conduct yourself on a daily basis is much more indicative of what you value than choosing words from a values list. You will want to search your life rather than your head. Much of this book is about feelings rather than about intellectualizing.

Just like in the exercise that helped you discover your purpose, think back to peak moments when life was especially rewarding. This time stay in those brief moments rather than moving on to the unfolding story (heart, not head). What was happening? Who was present? Which of your values were being honored?

To give you a bit of help I will list some words which describe certain values—just promise to remain in your heart and not analyze.

Accomplishment
Acknowledgment
Adventure
Aesthetics
Beauty
Community
Connectedness
Contribution
Creativity
Empowerment
Freedom
Growth
Harmony
Honesty

Independence
Integrity
Joy
Nurturing
Orderliness
Peace
Performance
Risk taking
Romance
Service
Spirituality
Success
Wealth

Of course, there are hundreds of words in English that could describe values. Those are just a few to give you an idea. Use whatever words work for you. Take note that your definition of a word will differ from someone else's.

Below, begin to list words that come to you as you recall those special peak moments.

(Music, maestro!)

1. ______________________
2. ______________________
3. ______________________
4. ______________________
5. ______________________
6. ______________________

7. ____________________
8. ____________________
9. ____________________
10. ____________________
11. ____________________
12. ____________________
13. ____________________
14. ____________________
15. ____________________
16. ____________________
17. ____________________
18. ____________________
19. ____________________
20. ____________________

Another exercise you can do to add words to your list is to look at what you must have in your life. Put aside the physical needs of food, shelter, and clothing and think of those things that fulfill you. Is it an absolute requirement for you to have love/romance, creativity/accomplishment, or organization/neatness? Towards what do you feel a constant urge to move? What are the values you must honor otherwise a part of you will die?

Add those words to the list above.

To turn the coin, think of things that get in your way of living according to your values. If something or someone caused you to feel distressed, describe that feeling. Could it be you felt controlled or fragmented? This could indicate your values of freedom and harmony were being trod upon.

Write down at least one time when you felt upset, and you can nail the word that describes how you felt. Then, look for the word that would portray what you felt was being taken from you. It will be a *value* for you.

Again, add the value or values to the list above.

One more exercise.

When you are in your bed in the nursing home, knowing that the time for you to pass on to the other side is near, what do you want going through your mind?

- I wish I'd earned a million dollars.
- I wish I'd had a home in the Cayman Islands.
- I wish I'd earned that promotion.
- I wish I'd not sold my grandmother's diamond earrings.
- I wish I'd traveled to Machu Picchu.
- I wish I'd been more honest with people.
- I wish I'd volunteered more.
- Regrets, regrets, and more regrets.

Or, I'm so grateful that my spouse and I had a date night once a week, that people could depend on me, that I helped empower others, that I supported those less fortunate than myself.

Regrets or gratitude?

This is a tough one, but it really slams home what it is that you value. The first three are just to show you how ridiculously important we often think these types of things are to us. In the end, are they really? I'm sure you will come up with more values in this exercise, so just add them to your list above.

Discovering your values can take some time. Now that you have awakened to the fact that you do have values and that they can be named, you will be more aware of them and over the next few weeks or months and will be able to define even more.

For now, if you have a list of 20, that is ideal, but in any case I'd like for you to take your list and cross out half, starting with those that have lesser importance than the half that will remain. If you have 20, you will cross out 10. This does not mean that these things are not values for you, they are just not as high on the list as those you did not cross out.

Not that easy, is it?

So let's do it again. Cut your remaining list in half. If you have 10, you will now have 5.

Wow, now that's tough, right?

If you started with 10, 20, or 30, it doesn't matter, just be sure you have five left.

Insert one of the remaining value words in the next sentence.

To me, ____(value)__________ means __(your definition)___________.

For example, I might create:

To me, organization means having a neat and orderly environment so that I can think and act in an orderly way, otherwise I feel scattered, stressed, and unable to focus.

Do this for each of your five value words.

I'm reminded of a husband and wife who, oddly enough, ended up with the same five words but when their individual definitions of those words were written, it showed they gave entirely different meanings. So these definitions are crucial to identifying your true values.

Lastly, study your value words and definitions. Choose the one of your highest value. Then, choose your next highest value, and the next, and so on until all five have been put in order.

Using any manner you wish, for example a fancy font, calligraphy, painting, drawing, make yourself something beautiful to hang on a wall or cherish privately in a journal or scrapbook that depicts your own unique values.

Yes, your values may change. As you mature and gain the wisdom that comes with age or find yourself in drastically altered circumstances, it is common for your values to change. The order changes too, and sometimes the definition or the value itself changes. However, you will note a commonality in your values throughout your life.

You have been working hard at this, but your reward is something to remind you of your specialness and the revelation of discovering more about who you are.

Congratulations!

Chapter Four

Left, Right, Left, Right

Right: The dictionary explains 'right' as the side of something that lies east when it is facing north, or the corresponding direction. *Lynn's Dictionary* explains it with the question, "Which way is north?"

A Greyhound bus trip it's not, but an adventurous experience it is. It takes 25 minutes to fly from Kathmandu to Pokhara. The bus trip takes 8 to 10 hours. Now, about the 'bus.' On the advice of our guide, Ganesh, we chose the 'microbus' rather than a public bus, because the microbus has seating for about 15 people and usually arrives a couple of hours earlier.

Early one morning, English Peter, English Chris, Ganesh, and I took a cab from our hotel to Kalanki, the area where the buses congregate. What meets our barely opened eyes is a very noisy, haphazard tangle of taxis, micro buses, larger buses, hollering people, street merchants, and what appears to be mass confusion. Our taxi motors slowly among the mess looking for a micro bus going to Pokhara. There is no way to know until you ask or hear someone yell, "Pokhara!"

At last we locate one, pay the fare, and Ganesh puts me in the window seat behind the driver, as he knows my tendency for claustrophobic fits in crowds and tight places. Now we wait. And wait and wait. It's well past departure time, but it seems we don't leave until every seat is full.

We finally do go – about 50 feet – and pull over. The driver hops out, and starts yelling "Pokhara!" Through my open window flies a fist holding a bottle of water, then another with some supposedly edible 'thing,' followed by a third fist clutching a newspaper, and on and on. After a few minutes, we finally get going – another 50 feet. We pull over, and the whole process starts again.

This running of the gauntlet continues even after the seats are full. It is now an hour past departure time. And guess what? The driver finds another four people to squeeze in the bus. I am now squashed up against the side of the bus, sitting sideways on one 'cheek,' with a cheek of the facial kind smushed on the window glass. But my window is large and if I had to, I could crawl out, so no claustrophobic panic yet.

Finally, we travel beyond 50 feet and our hearts lurch with hope. Yes, we keep on going! Sort of. Winding our way out of the city is a crawling stop-and-go, horn-honking melee. Finally, we reach the road to Pokhara which is, hallelujah, paved. After being in Kathmandu for a month, I suddenly realize something: it's left-side driving in Nepal. The mess of traffic in Kathmandu, weaving all over the narrow streets in and around all modes of transportation, muddies that issue.

We actually have two drivers, one behind the wheel and one on the roof with the luggage. Our upper driver bangs on the roof in what we assume is code to inform the inner driver of things like, "I hear a truck coming around that blind curve." The inner driver leans on the horn to announce our presence. In fact, all traffic hits the horn as it approaches every curve. I certainly hope drivers have to pass a hearing test.

On we go. It's hot. My open window saves my sanity, and I silently bless Ganesh. Air conditioning? Just a word in a foreign language never translated. We wind around the road and climb up and down and pass through small villages. In some, we stop and pick up another passenger or two, flattening the space hardly large enough for a box of rice. Speaking of which, we now see rice paddies in the terraced hills. The landscape is truly beautiful.

In one of these villages, we stop for lunch. I'm sure we resemble the circus Volkswagen which expels several dozen clowns from its tiny interior. My numb 'cheek' begins to prickle with life again as I limp over to the outdoor table on which I find several pots of completely unidentifiable (except for the flies) and supposedly edible concoctions. Appetite now dead, I purchase a bottle of Coke which seems the safest choice, plus it's cold.

Twenty minutes later, we do the clown trick in reverse, but the driver just sits with the motor running. Sweat runs in rivulets into my eyes—and stings!—on down my face and neck, and I'm hanging out the window gasping and praying for a breeze, and I couldn't care less what it smells like. Seems we are waiting for two passengers who have disappeared. Plenty of Nepali jabbering is going on between passengers and driver until we finally leave.

A half-hour later, a hand with a cell phone appears from above and in the driver's window. Seems the upper driver is also in charge of communications. We pull over and a conversation ensues. Don't have any idea what is being said, but the passengers are laughing and contributing their own opinions. Seems the two missing passengers finally showed up and found the bus gone. They had gone off down the road to eat elsewhere without telling the driver or asking how long they had to eat. And they wanted us to come back and get them. Hah! When water buffaloes pas de deux.

After another half-hour, another cell phone call and another roadside stop. This time, the errant passengers want their belongings left at the next village. OK, we can do that.

This roadway is very busy with trucks, buses, motorbikes, and cars. One sees insane driving antics, especially with motorbikes that are carrying at least two or three people. The driver must wear a helmet but not the passengers. There must be some logic in that somewhere, but it's not apparent to me. The final 30 km to Pokhara has us back to pothole navigation and is s-l-o-w going. The trip seems endless, but we finally arrive in Pokhara three hours later than planned. The idea of flying back after the weekend is now extremely tempting.

For the return trip, we are experienced. We know this game, and we are prepared! Once again, Ganesh gets me to the window seat behind the driver. English Chris and I are on a bench that sits three people, and we plant our butts squarely and vow not to move. In front of us, just behind the front seat, is a ledge for us to put our backpacks. There are several other passengers to load but, for some reason, this can't be done without several minutes of Nepali chattering, everyone talking over everyone else, a modulated tone of voice impossible. It sounds like everyone is yelling, but there isn't any anger. Eventually the bus is loaded.

As we go along, we keep picking up more passengers until the bench seat for three and the ledge in front of us is now holding eight people! We have to alternate knees with the person facing us. English Chris says he had a stranger's knee in his crotch most of the way home. But we did not give up a millimeter of our butt space! The others could sit on top of each other. This happens because the driver wants to make as much money per trip as possible, and the comfort of passengers comes fifth.

Oh, yes, and during both trips, Nepali and Indian music blared from the radio all . . . the . . . way.

As if it couldn't get worse, we found ourselves slowing down and stopping behind a line of traffic. And we sat. And we sat. And we sat. Eventually some traffic would come the other way, but only about five vehicles at a time. We would creep forward a few feet at long intervals. One and a half hours later, we were through the cause of the slowed traffic.

Here's one I doubt you will ever hear happening at home. It appears that the day before, a motorcyclist from this village was killed on the roadway in a hit-and-run. The villagers stopped traffic to collect money for his family. Now that's very thoughtful and an hour and a half of our time was for a good cause. Until we learned that only one-quarter of the collection actually goes to the family.

This time, our quick supper was a Coke and a bag of chips for me, and I learn that if the need is great enough, I can actually use one of the reeking pit-style toilets.

It's dark when we reach the outskirts of Kathmandu, and the streets are jammed with traffic trying to get in and out of the city. We creep along, stopping and starting for two more hours, either eating exhaust or closing the window and being poached. The entire return trip took 10 hours to travel about 200 km, double the usual time required. I forgot the Nepali mantra: Nothing is as it is supposed to be in Nepal!

Never, never, never, never again! In the extremely unlikely event that I find myself having to travel from Kathmandu to Pokhara, that 25-minute flight is the only way.

Pokhara was a superb experience for us. A lush, green little city nestled by a lake and surrounded by the majesty of the breathtaking Himalayas. Sigh!

Oh give me a home
Where the water buffalo roam
and the bats and the monkeys do play.
Where seldom is heard

an English word and the skies are
mountain-peaked all day.

Did I claim to be a poet?

Many times during the trip to Pokhara, I asked myself, "Where was your brain when you decided to take a bus rather than take a 25-minute flight, Lynn?" Obviously, I was operating from the left half of my gray matter and was stuck in practical mode due to the expense of flying over a bus ticket.

It would have been so much more fun to fly over the Himalayas, be awestruck by their majesty, see Pokhara from the air, and free up many hours to spend exploring, shopping, talking with people, and just absorbing this beautiful part of Asia. So right-brained!

So let's take a closer look at what all this fuss about right and left brain is about. Well, of course, you don't have two brains, but you do have two halves. And they are completely separated except for a small connection called the corpus callosum (I threw that big, scientific word in there to impress you), which is deep inside the brain and looks like an empty toilet paper tube filled with fiber-optic spaghetti.

Let's do a fun exercise to show ourselves just how wired and complicated our brains are.

How smart is your right foot? This little exercise comes from an orthopedic surgeon. It will boggle your mind and you will keep trying over and over to see if you can outsmart your foot.

1. While sitting where you are, lift your right foot off the floor and make clockwise circles.

2. Now, while doing this, draw the number '6' in the air with your right hand. Your foot will change direction! And there's nothing you can do about it. It's preprogrammed in your brain.

You and I both know how silly this is, but before the day is done, you are going to try it again if you haven't already done so. But it's fun, isn't it? Try it out on friends and family.

By the way, if you draw the number '6' with your left hand, you will be able to keep your right foot doing clockwise circles. It takes concentration, but you can do it.

Such are the mysteries of our brains. So much we don't yet understand.

So far in this book, I have had you getting out of your head and into your feelings in order to uncover your purpose, passion, mission, and values. Well, now it's time to get back into your head. Don't worry, I know how good it feels to get into your heart, and we will be back there soon.

The manner in which people will succeed in our world today and in the foreseeable future depends on *relationships*, and because most of our goals depend on our relationships with other people, understanding and using right- and left-brained characteristics puts you at an advantage.

Just past the middle of 2008, our world shifted dramatically, most obviously in the realm of economics. No doubt, we were in a mess financially and, at the time I'm writing near the end of 2009, we are and will be paying for government deficits for many years to come.

The financial mess is just the more obvious Shift. There is much more going on and, wonder of wonders, it is all good! What? It's OK, my marbles are still in an orderly formation in my left lobe and creating entertaining patterns in my right lobe so that everything is normal and I am sane. This global experience really is a shift of tremendous benefit.

It's as if we have made a card game out of life but have been playing with only the face cards, and someone has told us there are 43 more cards in the deck, including four aces—which are the best cards. So, even if we are unconscious of it, we, as human beings, are reassessing some of our values, opening up to a greater spirituality, and looking toward using more creativity and relationships both in business and personal life. The emphasis is on more mellow, intangible interests, while the racing drive to amass things and to succeed is slowing. Just think, a slower pace of life . . . ahh.

What we are actually doing is moving from the Information Age to the Conceptual Age, and it is every bit as world-changing as our move from the Agricultural Age to the Industrial Age. During the past three centuries, as we moved from farms to factories to the Internet, it has been the left-brained characteristics which have been most used, and necessarily so. The Conceptual Age will swing us over to the right-brained characteristics. Most importantly, we will learn how to engage both in balance.

I tell you this because this shift in consciousness is going to affect the kind of goals you choose for your future. It will affect the direction education will take for your children and grandchildren, your own choices for career goals, raising a child, selecting a partner, all the way from the types of movies you watch to the music you listen to. I've noticed changes in the goals people are choosing. An upsurge in the intangibles, like healing relationships finding more meaning in a purpose and values, desires to engage in philanthropy and the creative arts, like writing, clothing design, and music, and all careers that emphasize helping others. Naturally, the accumulation of wealth is always a popular goal, but it's what we do with that wealth that is changing.

More good news. We can't outsource creative talent and empathy, the main themes of the Conceptual Age. We can outsource information like research, form completion, auditing, and programming, but you can't outsource the talents of the writer, designer, musician, humorist, relationship coach, philosopher, or spiritualist. Do you think this fact could affect students' career choices today?

Do you know if you are more right-brained or left-brained?

The brain does have two physical hemispheres. The right hemisphere controls the left side of the body, and the left hemisphere controls the right side of the body. This explains why someone with an injury on the right side of the brain, such as a stroke, will exhibit symptoms on the left side of the body. If you think back to our foot exercise, we used our right foot and our right hand, but it was the left hemisphere calling the shots. When we kept the right foot circling and used the left hand to draw the number '6,' we were able to do it. It took some concentration and a learning curve, but we could do it. We are using both sides of our brain to do this. It shows that when we engage both hemispheres in balance, we can do what may have previously seemed impossible.

When it comes to our thinking, the left hemisphere is sequential, reality-based, specializes in text, uses language and words, is analytical, orderly, and logical, involved in the past or the future, and believes in separateness. The right hemisphere is simultaneous, random, specializes in context and ideas, is creative, thinks in pictures, is involved in the moment, sees the big picture, and is holistic. The left knows logic and the right knows about the world. Together, they are a powerhouse and, according to Daniel Pink in his book *A Whole New Mind*, it is that 'togetherness' we want to balance. I recommend this book; it is interesting and, believe it or not, entertaining.

So how do we affect the balance of the two hemispheres? First, let's find out where your brain is in the balance of right- and left-thinking characteristics. The Art Institute of Vancouver has a free online test that I suggest you complete to help you appreciate what will come. Just go to the Web site at:

---

www.wherecreativitygoestoschool.com/vancouver/left_right/rb_test.htm

---

Record your score here:

Left:_______________ Right_________________

Particularly important in all your relationship goals, from your partner or spouse, your family, to the person you chat with while waiting in one of those endless lines, to your business associates and clients, is *empathy*, that ability to imagine yourself in someone else's shoes and sense what they are feeling.

If you have leadership goals, leadership is all about empathy, which is needed to connect with and inspire people. Ever felt empathy coming out of your computer? I think not. It is empathy that makes us human. In fact, you would do well to mix a good amount of empathy with science if you have goals to have a career in the medical field in this newly forming world we have shifted toward. Doctors who get to know their patients as people and not just as symptoms or diseases will actually have a greater proportion of success in treating these patients successfully.

I think of the woman who was referred to a specialist for a colonoscopy. Now this is not a procedure anyone wishes to have performed. An outdoor summer concert under a starry night sky it is not. It is dreaded about as much as having to prepare your income tax forms only to find out you won't get a refund but will have to pay more.

She met the doctor in his office to discuss her case, how to prepare for the 'event,' and set the day and time. The doctor was very pleasant, put her at ease with a bit of humor, and answered her questions. A few weeks later after suffering a preparation procedure that our enemies could use as torture, she presented herself to the outpatient desk at the hospital. Soon she was lounging on a narrow, plastic-covered, and sandpaper-sheeted bed with one blanket barely large enough to cover what the hospital gown did not. A nurse quickly and adeptly inserted an IV needle and something enigmatic dripped slowly into her vein.

The room had several other similarly prepped individuals, all sharing the same look of terror. Medical experimentation in a prison camp popped into her mind. Finally! A friendly face appears. Her doctor has come in the room, wearing his scrubs, and holding a chart. She smiles and waves. He keeps on walking without as much as an eye twitch in her direction. She thinks, "That's OK. Maybe he just didn't recognize me right away. It has been a few weeks and, after all, we all look the same in here."

A few minutes later he returns in the other direction. He looks straight at her, and she thinks, "Now he knows who I am and will come and speak some words of comfort to put me at ease." The doctor looks away as if she was a blank wall and keeps on walking out of the room. The next patient is wheeled away to the 'chamber,' and our woman is left to try flipping through well-worn magazines while one-handed (IV in the other) and lying prone.

Time passes, and here comes the doctor again. He is chatting with the nurses and seems to be in a good mood (the last patient must not have put up too much of a fight). Again, he walks past and, again, the non-seeing glance. This occurs between each patient's roll down the 'last mile' until it comes to her turn.

Desperately looking forward to the doctor's pat on her arm, the use of her name, and perhaps a humorous word or two before he begins the assault on her body, she hyperventilates almost to the point of passing out, which she prays she will do.

Now among the sentinels of beeping, flashing, and hiccupping machines, she lays in her uncomfortable bed while a nurse tells her what they are about to do. Our woman is about to leap from her plasticized mattress and take off down the hall carrying her enigmatic IV bag in one hand and groping unsuccessfully for the flaps on her paper gown with the other, when she hears the nurses' blessed words, "And you will sleep through it all."

And thus she does. Later, she is returned to the ward and served a glass of juice and a cookie which, after three days of nothing but blah broth and water, tastes like crème brûlée and champagne.

What do you think our woman remembers most about her experience? Not the preparation, not the charming holding room, not the most welcomed unconsciousness during the procedure, but the fact that her doctor, the person with whom she trusted her body, did not speak one word to her nor acknowledge her in any way. He could have been one of the machines. He did not employ any empathy for his patient.

Can you empathize with her? Can you put yourself in her gown and feel what she felt? This involves using your right brain.

Perhaps you will need empathy to choose the correct goals for yourself or you will need to use it continually once your goal is achieved, e.g., earning a degree in family law, counseling, social work, nursing, medicine, teaching, raising a family, getting married, or any activity or work that involves being with people. And there's not much that doesn't.

You can test your empathy quotient on this Web site:

---

www.glennrowe.net/BaronCohen/EmpathyQuotient/EmpathyQuotient.aspx

---

How often have you thought, "If I just had . . . " or "When I get . . ." or "After I get . . ."? So much of our goal setting is involved in accumulation. Remember, as a teenager, you were so certain that if you could just have that certain pair of shoes, that first car, or those name brand jeans, etc., then life would be forever wonderful. If you got your heart's desire, then life was wonderful—but not forever, because before long, the nirvana of receiving what you so desperately wanted wore off only to be replaced by a new heart's desire. This continues throughout our lives, not just in the teen years.

Why do you think that is? Viktor Frankl, in his book *Man's Search for Meaning*, says, "Man's main concern is not to gain pleasure nor to avoid pain, but to see a meaning in his life." This search for meaning is a natural drive all humans experience. We are almost always motivated by gaining pleasure or avoiding pain, but these are just the boulders in the stream while the flowing water is the motivation to find meaning for what we do and why we are here.

Accumulation of material possessions is left-brained while meaning is right-brained. Imagine if you could walk into a shop and purchase 500 grams of meaning. I imagine it would carry a hefty price, as it would be much sought after; therefore, you could only afford to purchase a small amount at a time. It would be as if you could purchase your 'purpose,' such as we discussed in a previous chapter.

Well, perhaps it's a good thing we cannot buy the thing we most search for, because then it would become just another commodity and like any other commodity that devalues in our eyes as time passes instead of increasing in value.

When we stock up on souvenirs during that long yearned for cruise, what are we really buying? Not the T-shirt blazoned with the name of the cruise line, not the beach towel with Barbados printed in large letters across its surface, not the dozen pictures you purchased from the ship's photographer, and not the sombrero the size of the Yucatan. You are hoping that when you see and touch these things in the years to come, you will recapture the moments of pleasure, laughter, and relaxation, the sound of the ocean, the tastes of sumptuous meals, the beat of the music, and the feel of the ship slipping through the quiet waters as you gazed at a night sky punctuated with lustrous stars and a hovering moon just over the horizon. The souvenirs are your accumulations, all else is meaning.

And so it seems we accumulate in order to find meaning in these objects. We buy things, we change our surroundings, change our appearances, change our partners, change our jobs and careers, and all the time we are searching for a meaning behind it all. Most of us don't know that's what we are doing.

Here's yet another reason why this shift in consciousness is such a blessing. We are ever so slowly, yet surely awakening to the realization that our priorities are changing. We live in such abundance that we no longer have to do backbreaking work from dawn to dusk, thus we have more time to contemplate our existence. Knowledge is at our fingertips on a keyboard, in lending libraries, on CDs and DVDs, and we are seeking that knowledge.

We are becoming more spiritual in that we have a deeper sense of the purpose of our existence and a belief that something larger than us is present. Movies such as *What the Bleep Do We Know?* show us how quantum physics and faith-based factions are really talking the same language. *The Secret* zeros in on the power of just one of the Universal Laws. Neale Donald Walsh has *Conversations with God* and writes about them to the tune of one best-selling book after another. In a past age, he would have suffered a tortuous death for blasphemy—that's how far we have come.

We are eager to learn, and that is why these books, movies, and words by masters such as Wayne Dyer, Marianne Williamson, Gary Zukov, Eckhart Tolle, Sylvia Browne, Jack Canfield, Jerry and Esther Hicks, and so many other enlightened individuals are made famous by the sheer numbers of people buying their materials and experiencing positive changes in their lives.

Have you ever walked through a labyrinth? My first knowledge of a labyrinth and its purpose was during a time when my sister and I were touring around Vancouver Island's cozy little hidden-away treasure spots, and we stopped at a lavender farm. While strolling among the fragrant fields, we came across a labyrinth that had been laid out on the ground using stones. It is a circular-patterned path that coils inward to its center, much like a rope on the deck of a ship. My sister explained to me that it was a method of walking meditation. Our left brain is busy with the logistics of the path which leaves our right brain free to be in the moment.

Now that I know about labyrinths, I have learned there are thousands of them, both private and public, around the world. People are designing them in their back yards or on the roofs of apartment buildings. If you lack a space, you can draw one on paper and walk it with your fingers.

From where does the hunger for these things come? It seems to have been wired into our right brain, the part of our brain that has not been in the forefront during the past century. Frankly, I think our left brain has simply gotten fed up with carrying the load for so long and has thrown up its hands in resignation and hollered over the bridge of the corpus callosum to its nonidentical twin on the right, "Take over for a while, will you? I'm going for a nap."

One thing is certain. Life in the right brain is fun, which now means we will be enjoying such a good time, most of the time, in our present and future. If you don't feel you are there yet, not to worry, some of us just have that need to push to the head of the line.

It's all about choosing those goals. And here I am going to break one of the fundamental (left-brained) laws of Goaling. We have been taught to be specific and detailed in the visualization and descriptions of our goals, that the Big Universe cannot give us what we want if it doesn't have specifics. Well, I say you can set a goal for something general.

Look at it this way. The Big U is an all-knowing, omnipotent energy. It created itself, after all! Do you think it just may know more than what our two-sided brain, of which we use only 10%, can conjure up? It will send us what we need, even though sometimes that will be a cause for much confusion on our part—it may not even make sense at the time. Just give it time, because it will. You may think fun is a Mediterranean cruise, but your Source knows it is learning ballroom dancing! Now if you are a left-brained control freak, you may be scared cross-eyed. Left brainers have a more difficult time with surrender. I know. I am one.

A new equation to Goaling has been added. It's about surrender and trust. If your goal is for more fun, more passion, more creativity, and more emotional freedom, these are right-brained characteristics and it's likely you may not know how to find them, otherwise you would already have them. So why not surrender and remain open for what is delivered? We are told to ask and not be concerned with the how-to when we go Goaling. To me, that looks like contradiction. Do we get specific or do we let ourselves be unconcerned with how? I actually use both in my coaching. If a goal is emanating from the left brain, I get specific. But if a goal is right-brained oriented, I encourage surrender and trust.

And here I thought getting to Pokhara was so left-brained. You know, a schedule, an assigned seat, one person to a seat, a lunch that was recognizable, and a butt that didn't take an hour to get its circulation back in action. The left brain is not all that busy in Nepal.

In the next chapter, you will see just what my Source had in store for me and what ended up being the 'reason' I was to go to Nepal. I could not have specified this if I spent every waking moment for the rest of my life thinking about it.

Resources
A Whole New Mind, Daniel Pink

Stroke of Insight, Jill Bolte Taylor,
http://www.ted.com/talks/jill_bolte_taylor_s_powerful_stroke_of_insight.html

Right Brain vs. Left Brain Creativity Test, Art Institute of Vancouver
http://www.wherecreativitygoestoschool.com/vancouver/left_right/rb_test.htm

Empathy Quotient Test, Glenn Rowe
http://glennrowe.net/BaronCohen/EmpathyQuotient/EmpathyQuotient.aspx

Chapter Five

Soul Connection

Connection: The dictionary defines 'connection' as something that links two or more things. *Lynn's Dictionary* defines it as eye contact.

A typical Kathmandu day in the life of this transplanted volunteer English-teaching Westerner would go like this:

The cheeping of the battery-powered travel alarm clock would wake me at an early hour, and I would roll out of bed, prep myself for the day ahead, and climb a flight of stairs to the top floor of the hotel to the kitchen where Deepak would politely ask me what I would like for breakfast. I would sit out on the patio deck high above the street below and enjoy the morning sun as I ate my toast and eggs and drank a sweet coffee that was something akin to a latte at home.

With my Nepali shoulder bag stuffed with teaching aids with lesson plans from the night before, a two-liter bottle of water, an umbrella (for protection from the sun, the occasional shower, or an aggressive stray dog) and my iPod, I would strike out from the Thamel area on the five-km walk to Sangye Choling Monastery in the Swayambhu area. I dodge rickshaws, taxis, pedestrians, carts, buses, motorcycles, doggy do-do, and garbage along the narrow streets that lack sidewalks. Within one block, I begin to sweat from the humidity and the rising temperature. I learned early on not to rush and, therefore, I take nearly an hour to reach my destination, the final third a tough uphill climb.

I would have enough time before class to sit under a tree in the monastery courtyard, hopefully feel a bit of breeze, drink a liter of water, and perhaps chat with one or two of the monks while using a package of tissues to mop my face, neck, arms, and soaking hair. Then, I would take the stairs down to the cooler basement classroom to be greeted by 25 little six- to ten-year-old voices hollering, "Good morning, miss!" and "Namaste!"

With a continual tide of volunteer English teachers from every English-speaking country coming and going in Nepal, the little monklettes (my term) had a pretty good understanding of English, although I still did a good amount of miming, gesticulating, and making funny faces, which entertained them to no end. They had different levels of English-speaking abilities, making teaching both a challenge and a blessing as the better English students could help the others. There were no desks, and everyone sat cross-legged on the floor. However, there was one plastic chair for the teacher and a white board and markers. I spent most of my time on the floor anyway.

Young boys are the same the world over. Rambunctious! Not having reached the stage yet in Buddhism where they become soft-spoken, respectful, smiling, nodding, and peace-loving, they were wild for the felt colors and coloring books I brought, the Scrabble tiles, the game prizes, and books. When an assignment was completed, they crowded around me, shoving their papers at me all yelling "Finished! Finished! Finished!" until I took their papers and penciled stars on them. I barely had room to breathe. Soon, the hour was gone and we would form our 'goodbye' circle. I would say a few words about the day's lesson, we would namaste each other, and I would hear a chorus of "See you tomorrow!" as they ran off to their next activity.

I would then climb stairs to the top floor of the monastery for my second class, which consisted of boys about 16 years old who were much quieter, more studious, and at various levels of English. The view across Kathmandu from the windows was breathtaking! I would often stand at an open widow and feel like Julie Andrews in *The Sound of Music* when she flung open the windows and burst into song: "The hills are alive with the sound of music!" I didn't burst into song out of respect for any ears in hearing distance.

This was a very enjoyable class. Their favorite activity was the jigsaw puzzle of Canada I had brought with me. The first jigsaw puzzle they had ever encountered, they did not want to stop at the end of the hour and, in fact, returned later in the evening to finish before class the next day. I used the opportunity to teach them about Canada, the provinces, capital cities, industries, etc. I even taught the few words of French I remember from high school. They were fascinated by the process of making maple syrup.

After class, Tenzin Lama, the head of education at the monastery, would bring me a cold drink of some exotic Nepali liquid, such as Fresca or Coke, and it did taste like nectar! And then I would be off for the trek back to the hotel, go out for lunch with other volunteers, and then spend the afternoon and evening exploring shops, the city, its surroundings, in an Internet cafe, and lesson planning for the following day.

Then, my whole experience took a dramatic turn.

One day, as I was returning from teaching at the Monastery, I glanced at a heap of garbage by the side of the street (one of many, due to a garbage strike) and uttered a groaning gasp as I witnessed a small dog, one very different from the average street dog, desperately digging for any morsel of food.

She was missing three-fourths of her fur, and what was left was so filthy one could not be sure of the color. She was wounded, her skin was covered with rashes, and it was obvious that she had had a litter of pups not too long ago. The vast majority of street dogs are male, since the females keep having litters when sick and malnourished and, therefore, die sooner. I took a video of the scene thinking I would somehow use it to bring attention to the huge stray dog population issue in Kathmandu. I went on my way, but with a heavier heart.

It was raining the following day as I slogged my way to classes in my neon-orange boots and pink plastic poncho. And there, in the same general area as the day before, stood this wee, soaking wet, shivering dog. These stray dogs usually keep away from people and won't look at them. But both times, she looked straight at me with sad, helpless, confused, pleading brown eyes, and tears spilled from my own eyes. From that moment, she never left my heart or my head.

Later that day, as I showered off the sweat (I still sweat even when it rains!), I had an epiphany. I scare myself with these dang epiphanies! The last one was when I said to myself, "I'd love to go to Nepal and teach English to Buddhist monks!" This one said, "I must rescue that dog!" Oh, groan, another goal just found me.

And so the die was cast. I hardly slept that night, what with worrying that I would not find her again now that I had committed to rescuing her. I did not see her on the way to classes the next day. Coming back, she was not in her usual area. I began pleading really hard with the doggie angels and, about a block later, there she was. It seems once you make a commitment, the Source steps in and you have a silent partner. I had already named her Atma, and that was the first word that shot out of my mouth: "Atma! There you are!"

Keeping one eye on her, I ran to a shop and asked for a cardboard box, and was emphatically turned down even when I explained in Pidgin English that I wanted it to rescue that dog. Undaunted, I went next door and pleaded again for a box. This time, I was rewarded by a kind-hearted man. I had brought food, and I placed it in the box as I sat on a step beside her and talked soothingly. She let me stroke the top of her head with one finger as I watched a flea population equal to the size of Mt. Everest race over her bare body parts and thinly covered areas with what I would later discover, should have been white fur.

Now I'm thinking, if I try to pick her up and put her in the box, she may bite me, and the flea situation was an even stronger deterrent. Then there appeared a Nepali angel. A man of senior years managed to ask me, through sign language and unintelligible words, if I wanted the dog in the box. When I finally understood and vigorously nodded my head, he just picked her up and put her in the box. Nothing to it! Better him than me. We closed the flaps, and one would have thought we had captured the Tasmanian Devil! We needed rope . . . and fast! He skittered off, came back with some plastic twine, and with much grunting and dexterity we managed to tie the flaps in place, looking at each other with big grins.

By now we had quite an audience, and I managed to make it known that I was going to take her to an animal hospital. Someone hailed a taxi for me and with plenty of jabbering between bystanders and driver, he managed to understand where I wanted to go. I struck a deal for the cab fare, and off we went.

This animal hospital could only give me prescriptions for what Atma needed, and I was to take her home and administer the drugs. I'm looking at the flea colony and shaking my head adamantly. Seems they had no facilities at this clinic for keeping her there. And by now, she's figured out the box flip lid equation, popping out her little head with a body desperately wanting to follow. I only stopped this by picking up the first thing within reach, which happened to be a bundle of just delivered newspapers, that I grabbed with one hand and dumped on the top of the box and leaned on.

I was given an address of another animal hospital, this time a private clinic, and yet again a cab was hailed for me. I make a deal for the fare once more, and we are off across the city a second time. I wonder if the first clinic ever missed that new bundle of newspapers.

The potholes and broken pavement make for a rough ride, with me desperately hanging on to a slipping newspaper pile. The appearance now and then of a frightened eyeball through a space between the box flaps tells me I'm not too successful.

When we arrive at the Animal Hospital and Research Centre of Kathmandu, I juggle a wiggling box and rapidly flying newspapers to the reception area and gratefully plunk down on a seat, gasping with effort. The popping head emerges once more from the box placed on the floor, and the whole thing strikes me as hysterical. I simply have to take a video of Atma's jack-in-the-box antics with her defiantly rumpled appearance (could she look even worse?), box, newspapers, et al.

This time, an examination administered by a vet trained in the Netherlands shows that her skin problem and lack of fur is dermatitis produced by the fleas and can be easily cleared up with medication. When I tell him I am in a hotel, he orders a flea and tick bath to do away with that problem. She has two shots to prevent any flea return, to do away with any worms, to heal her skin and relieve her need to scratch. Spaying and vaccinations can be done ten days later if her health is good.

I'm given a 'clean' box, which she again vigorously fights against being placed inside, and we end up in the cab going home as a team of one thoroughly disheveled woman and a triumphant dog, head free of the box. We actually struck a deal, but she thought she had won.

Why the name Atma? It is the Nepali word for soul, because from the moment we first made eye contact, we made a Soul Connection.

"There is one great truth on this planet: whoever you are, or whatever it is that you do, when you really want something, it's because that desire originated in the soul of the Universe. It's your mission on earth."
— Paulo Coelho, The Alchemist

"How do you know when you have made a Soul Connection?" is the most common question I am asked about this subject. It's when that small voice within becomes that big voice within. Your Divine Source never hollers. Just as your Guardian Angel whispered your purpose in your tiny newborn ear, your inner voice is always calm and gentle. It is just as if you heard it while standing next to Big Ben when it struck the hour.

You feel it rather than hear it. It is part of being your life as opposed to doing your life. When you are doing life, you are being responsible, focused, intentional, and you want to make something happen. When you are being life, you are immersed in life's flow, letting go, accepting, allowing, blending with life's motion.

We can pretty much say the Soul Connection feeling is right-brained (being life). Most often when it occurs, your left brain leaps in and begins swiftly listing the reasons you either did not feel what you felt or the justifications as to why the message you received is not doable (doing life). For a whole approach to accomplishing your goals, you need to be aware of both doing and being. For now, we are concentrating on being life.

Let's play a game. I'm going to take you on a walk. You are on a path in a lovely forested area. The sun is shining through the leaves and the branches of the trees are letting through dappled touches of light on the forest floor. As you round a bend on this path, you are suddenly face-to-face with a bear.

Now write: What do you do?

____

____

____

And why do you do it?

____

____

____

You have managed to elude the bear and continue along on your journey. As you glance around at your surroundings, you see something shiny on the ground. You bend to pick it up and discover it is a key.

Describe the key: What does it look like?

____

____

____

What do you do with it?___________________________

____

____

The key looked after, you continue on your way. It isn't long before you make another discovery. This time, you find a cup sitting by the side of the path.

Describe the cup: What does it look like?

____

____

____

What do you do with it?

____

____

____

You find the path widening somewhat, and you are surprised to discover water before you.

What does this water look like?

____

____

____

What do you do there?

____

____

____

You now leave the water and carry on until you come to a wall.

What does this wall look like?

____

____

____

At the wall, what do you do?

____

____

____

This experiment can be just a fun game that you can play with other people, and you will find that some answers to the questions can be very funny. Comparing answers with each other can be revealing as well. The water can be a lovely lake where one can wade tired feet in cool water, while another's water can be a scummy pond full of frogs.

What I would like you to do in the context of our subject is to look at your answers and decide if ugliness or fear is present. Were you terrified at encountering the bear? Was the key rusty and old? Was the cup dirty and broken? Was the water ugly? Was the wall insurmountable? Be truthful, no one will know but you.

Look at your answers again. This time, look for peace or beauty. Did you stand quietly and stare down the bear or wave your arms and scream loudly, "I know you can hurt me, but I know you won't because I don't want to hurt you either"? To the best of my knowledge, making loud noises and doing anything to make you look larger is one recommended way to scare off a bear. Another is to be very still and maintain eye contact until the bear walks away. Just thought I'd throw that in should you ever encounter a bear.

Now, was the key ornate, shiny, or magical? The cup like a chalice or a porcelain tea cup? The water an ocean during sunset or a trickling stream winding among moss-covered rocks? Did your wall have a door? Was this wall one-foot high or six-feet long? Was it made of grass or stone?

Beside the answers you have written, write one of these words: fear, ugly, beauty, and peace. If one of those doesn't fit, write your own word and pay attention to how you *feel* when you write it.

Now we want to determine if you were coming from Ego or Spirit with your answers.

At any given time, we are living in either Ego or Spirit.

We all have an Ego, and its actual purpose is to protect us. But because it wants to remain in control, it becomes over-protective to the point where you can become fearful of almost anything. It can protect you from jumping into deep water if you can't swim, or it can cause you to be afraid of learning how to swim. It can protect you by reminding you to put out a burning candle before you sleep, or it can cause you to be so afraid of fire that you awake several times in the night to see if you smell smoke.

The Ego can protect you from disappointment by convincing you not to set goals because they might not be fulfilled. The Ego keeps you in judgment, which is really a fear that you aren't good enough, one of the most prevalent and most insidious fears among us.

Of course, your Ego is intangible. To me, my ego is every fearful thing, every limited belief that was ever instilled in me (more on this in a later chapter). It keeps me from being the spiritual entity that I am. It keeps me asking questions that begin, "What if?" out of fear and not out of personal growth.

On the other hand, when we look at being in Spirit, we have a knowingness that we are not separate from each other, our world, or our Universe. The Ego is all about separateness. Each one of us has an effect on everything and everyone else. We are all connected, having come from the same source, and that source is pure love.

That random act of kindness you perform for someone is also performed for yourself. When you give to others, you give to yourself. Love others, and you love yourself. Be patient with others, and you are patient with yourself. Be understanding of others, and you understand yourself. Being 'in Spirit' keeps you in giving mode, which is really love; whereas, being 'in Ego' keeps you in judgment mode, which is really fear and separation.

Now, revisit your notes on your walk in the forest. This time, put the words 'Ego' or 'Spirit' beside each of your answers. Pay particular attention to how you instantly feel when you read your answers.

As an example, let's look at your key. Maybe it was a bright, shiny, brand-new car key with a microchip in it. This can be looked at in either Ego mode or Spirit mode. In Ego mode, the key may represent that you feel judgmental of the person who lost it by thinking, "How could anyone be so inept as to lose their key here? I bet they will be angry when the car won't start. No way to know who it belongs to, so I'll just leave it here." In Spirit mode, we may think, "Gee, it's a good thing this key is so shiny or I may not have seen it. It couldn't have been here very long, so I'll pick it up and take it with me. Maybe I'll find the owner up ahead or I can turn it in somewhere."

In the first example, in Ego mode, can you feel how this thinking separates the key finder from the key loser? How the key finder has a sense of superiority over the key loser? In Spirit mode example, can you sense that this person is connected with another person on an empathetic level? That this key finder wants to help the key loser just as he/she would want someone to help him/her in similar circumstances?

In essence, any time you have an uncomfortable or uneasy feeling about any situation, you can be sure Ego is involved somewhere, either yours or someone else's. When circumstance finds you feeling happy, smiling, in admiration, grateful, etc., you know that Spirit is present.

As you do this part of the exercise, if you find that you were in Ego mode somewhere in the game, don't be judgmental or harsh with yourself . . . that would be staying in Ego mode! Every one of us continually switches modes. We are human beings, not perfect beings. The purpose of this game is to help reveal your tendency towards fear and Ego or trust, love, and Spirit. If it is the former, no worries. You have uncovered something about yourself. If you are unhappy with that knowledge, you can change. The important thing is for you to acknowledge it, because until you acknowledge something, you can't change.

A wonderful tool is learning to quiet your mind through meditation, not only in helping you make the changes you want to make but also in getting you closer to feeling and 'hearing' a Soul Connection with your Source.

Being in Spirit mode is so important when it comes to your Soul Connection goals. If you have been afraid to set goals, think about from where this fear is coming. You were not born with this fear. In fact, you were born with only two fears: falling and loud noises. All the rest of your fears are learned through either experience or by the words of other people.

Your Divine Source teaches only love. It wants you to feel fulfilled, live your dreams, and be in a position to help others. It wants you to feel your connection with it and be able to tune yourself to its guidance. It does not want you to bury your light under a heap of fear. You are no good to yourself or others or this planet by being that way. Your Divine Source wants you to have intentions. Trust that it will guide you to the right ones.

An essential part of life is to fulfill your Purpose by aspiring to attain your goals. You are created to dream and to grow and to be fulfilled just as much as you are created to walk and to breathe and to think. If you are not experiencing joy in accomplishing your dreams by establishing and attaining your goals, you are leaving behind a huge part of the best of life.

What's important for you to know is you *can* be a goal setter. You *can* be a goal achiever. All you may need is guidance, support, some new tools, and a cheerleader. All of this is available to you. Just ask the Universe, and the right person will be delivered to you.

Resources

1. There is much more to be learned about Ego and Spirit, and two of my favorite books are:

A New Earth, Eckhart Tolle

The Moses Code, James Twyman

2. When I work in person with clients, we can be more specific in finding the right tools to assist a person shifting to Spirit mode. Every person is unique, so there can be no cookie-cutter formula to fit everyone.

To assist you further, I am providing an article on the deeper meaning of the bear, the key, the cup, the water, and the wall exclusively for readers of Inspirational Goaling. Go to http://www.inspirationalgoaling.com/trailwalk and use the code **'game'**. You will discover much more about yourself in your answers.

3. To assist with visualization meditation, I offer a free audio file for download by readers of Inspirational Goaling. My voice will personally guide you on a visit to your future self, the person you will be when you have attained some of your most desired goals. To download the audio file, go to http://www.inspirationalgoaling.com/meditation and use the code **'visit'**.

Chapter Six

Law and Order

Law: The dictionary defines 'law' as a binding or enforceable rule. *Lynn's Dictionary* defines it as the Laws of Man – far too left-brained as compared to the Laws of the Universe, which are magnificent!

I left you with Atma and me getting back to the hotel after her flea bath and medications at the Animal Hospital and Research Centre of Kathmandu. She was a sorry sight with no hair over three-fourths of her body, her bare skin covered in a rash. Nonetheless, she was introduced to my fellow volunteers and the hotel staff, many of whom must have wondered what the heck I had seen in her.

But as the next few days went by, Atma wriggled her way into many of their hearts just as she had crashed into mine. What she had looked like faded away, and all one could see of her was her amazing little spirit shining from her eyes. Her name, Atma, is the Nepali word for soul.

We quickly discovered that she was not about to allow me out of her sight. The whining, barking, scratching, and mournful dog language that echoed throughout the hotel when I left her alone in the room made it clear that she was going to be attached to me like gum on a shoe for the duration of my time in Nepal.

So off we went to teach at the monastery every morning. She sat on the plastic chair, and was every bit the lady with all her monklettes doting on her. After class, we trotted back to the hotel. She drank a small ocean of water while her mum showered, and then out to lunch we would go. We chose outdoor garden restaurants where she was welcome, and after the morning's walking workout, she would curl up on a seat beside me and never move.

She trotted along my left side after I made her a leash and collar out of a shoulder bag strap and a safety pin. It's obvious she had been leash-trained or else she is just a very smart dog. She would entertain us by shaking her right then left paws alternately, dancing on her hind legs with forelegs making the namaste gesture, wanting to go outside to do bathroom duties, and listening to me with much more attention than any of my kids ever did. When I talk to her, she looks me right in the eyes. It's a bit disconcerting at first, because most dogs won't do that, but it's as if she understands every word I say. Who's to say she doesn't?

At night, she pops up on her comfy chair to sleep and stays there until the alarm wakes us. Then, I pat the spot on the bed beside me, and she leaps across the room, dives in beside me, and wriggles in for a morning pre-breakfast snuggle.

My Aussie friend Charmaine took on the chore of pseudo-mum while I went on my preplanned excursion to Pokhara—never have I had such a welcome reception upon my return! Face, glasses, and hair all received a thorough little-dog-tongue washing amid doggy squeals, helicopter tail whirling in a blur, and nonstop wiggles.

Now, it's time to get down to the business of getting her home with me. Talking to the airlines, finding a proper leash, collar, food, and a transportation kennel would take one day at home. In Kathmandu, it takes one week. But I am a new mama and am not to be deterred! We traverse the city in cabs, spend much time on the phone, go through rupees like starving bunnies in a lettuce field, but at last all is done except revisiting the vet.

It's time for her to be spayed and vaccinated. I drop her off in the late morning and receive instructions to come back around 6:00 p.m. I arrive on time and tiptoe to a room where she is lying in an old-fashioned metal baby crib. Still coming out of anesthetic, her eyes are slightly open but not focused, and her tongue is lolling out of her mouth. I speak quietly to the staff and the next thing I hear is a thump-thump-thump. She heard my voice and thumped her tail three times while absolutely nothing else on her body twitched—not even an eyelash! It was so sweet my throat lumped up.

Very gradually, she becomes more awake.

And then, everything changed . . . .

It seemed as though the light switch for the sun had been turned off and my world darkened. I felt I was teetering on the edge of a precipice and was powerless to stop it.

The newspapers beneath her body absorbing her urine were being changed frequently by an assistant when suddenly the urine started showing pink and then red. Atma was bleeding from somewhere. Two vets and three assistants materialized instantly to assess her.

Having no history on a street dog, it could have been a blood condition, such as hemophilia, or a urinary cyst that ruptured or, or, or! Dr. Yadav checked for cysts, went over every detail of the surgery, looked at her gums, which had turned white, and then injected her with iron and vitamin K. At this point, all we could do was wait and hope the bleeding would slow and then stop. The five staff members and I stood quietly around Atma, watching diligently for change, saying our own silent prayers.

At one point I was alone with her for a few minutes. And it was then that I felt a peacefulness come over me. My anxiety and worry calmed as I surrendered them to the Universe. I recalled the words of my first mentor, Val, when he said, "Our world may seem to be in chaos, but it is really unfolding in Lawful Order." For the first time I realized that these wise words did not just refer to our planet, but to each of us in our own life, which is our individual world. My thoughts had been tumbling in chaos as I felt so powerless and fearful during Atma's crisis. I was now reminded of the immutable Laws of the Universe and that I needed to align myself with them if I was to be of any help to Atma, the staff, or myself.

She needed to feel my peacefulness and not my anxiety, and so I cupped her chin in my hand, leaned down, and whispered in her ear, "Atma, you have such a strong little spirit and between you, me, and the help of our friends here in the hospital, we are all going to work as one to keep you with us. You were meant to come home with me, so keep fighting to stay with me and I will not leave you."

Within a half hour, the bleeding slowed and finally stopped. Everyone let out a communal sigh of relief at the good news and adjusted our prayers to ask that it not start again.

Even though within the next couple of hours I was assured that I could leave, every time I left the room Atma would fuss, move too much, and exhibit her separation anxiety and perhaps starting the bleeding again. So, true to my word, I did not leave her and stayed beside her for the night.

Atma and I were not the only ones in the room; we had a persistent visitor! Every time I put my head down on her bed to catch a few winks, bzzz, whine, bzzz, whine, a blasted mosquito started circling my ear. I could never find it, due to the subdued lighting in the room, and besides, I didn't want to smack the wall and disturb Atma. The mozzie didn't differentiate between my left and right ears either. I wouldn't see it for an hour, but as soon as I put my head down it was at my ear. I smacked myself stupid that night hoping to smush it on the side of my head.

I finally get back to the hotel at about 6:00 a.m. I return to the vet at about 5:00 p.m., and Atma is well enough to jump into my arms and give me the ol' Atma face wash routine. She had been given a 48-hour pain medication at the time of surgery, so she felt no discomfort. And back to the hotel we went, where she was spoiled by everyone, pampered by me, and allowed to sleep in my bed cuddled up and happy.

Three days later, she had a vet checkup. The cause of the bleeding was attributed to poor nutrition while Atma was on the streets, and her liver was unable to produce enough blood clotting material. She was given rabies, distemper, and parvo vaccinations, and she wiggled and licked her thanks to some incredibly caring and talented Nepali people. She was given the green light to travel. Big sigh! And a prayerful thank-you to the Big U.

"Every idea and mental picture must produce after its own kind whether the picture is good or bad; the Law determines it so"
— Raymond Holliwel, Working with the Law

There are the Laws of Man. We fallible humans make laws for reasons, from staunching anarchy and controlling crime, to local bylaws enforcing the size of signage and the time allowed to park your car in a particular area. I swear that in every level of government there is a person in a cubicle somewhere that is paid to create ridiculous laws. This is followed by those whose job it is to enforce these laws and mete out punishment for breaking them.

Our society is not perfect, and we are not perfect. Therefore, we will have imperfect laws, and they will always be in a state of flux and change. It can drive a person nuts! We have elections, referendums, and laws we hate and laws we love depending on our own way of thinking. We write letters to editors, government representatives, prime ministers, and presidents. Arguments go on in legislatures, senates, congresses, parliaments, courts, and city halls. It is the System, and it's flawed, but it's what we have and most humans do their best to obey the Laws of Man.

By contrast, we also have the Laws of the Universe, the Universal Laws. They have been in existence since time began and have never altered in any way. One can put faith in these laws because they are immutable. One does not hire a lawyer and go to court when they break a Universal Law. There is never a punishment, except for the self-induced reaction of not living with that particular law. No judge, no jury, no lawyer, no court. And most people aren't even aware of these laws let alone living in accordance with them.

Compared to the convoluted Laws of Man, the Laws of the Universe are refreshingly simple. Let me give you some examples.

- Either master your mind, or your mind will master you.
- Whether you like it or not, understand it or not, the Law is always there.
- Ideas emanate extraordinary energy.
- Whatever picture you carry in your mind is what is given to you, both negative and positive.

And I could go on for many pages.

When it comes to striving for your goals, take heed: those who understand and work aligned with Laws of the Universe will always succeed. Read that sentence again, write it down in big letters, and post it all over your home.

I don't know anyone who has not heard of the smash hit film *The Secret,* but I'm sure there are a few. The subject is a Universal Law named the Law of Attraction. Those who set out to put this Law to use and did not get the results they expected simply did not work in concert with *all* the laws. Which is likely not their fault, because they were not aware that there are at least 11 more of these laws. Think of it, only having to obey a dozen laws, and the beauty is that if you live in tandem with these 12 laws, you are automatically obeying most of the really important Laws of Man!

Now I'm going to disclose a fact of my own belief. **The Laws of Man are entirely the left-brained creations, whereas the Laws of the Universe are entirely right-brained.** If we think of the gravitational force at work on our planet, it's very tangible, we can see the results of ignoring it. Just look around at how creative man has had to be in order to live in accord with gravity. We must be aware of it every moment of our lives or face the consequences if we ignore it. It is exactly the same with the intangible Laws of the Universe, as you will soon see.

The Law of Thinking

As difficult as it may be for some people to trust in the intangibles, this is a requirement when it comes to these laws of life. Once you take your first steps in living in alignment with the Laws of the Universe, your experiences and results will continue to help you in solidifying that trust.

It begins with the belief that your thoughts are energy.

Write a negative thought that creeps into your head regularly.

____

____

____

Read what you have written and say it out loud at least 10 times. How do you feel? What happened to your body? Did you sigh at least once as you repeated this thought? Look what it did to your energy.

Now write a positive thought that regularly comes into your head.

____

____

____

As above, repeat it out loud at least 10 times. Now how do you feel? What happened to your body? Are you sitting or standing straighter? Are you more relaxed? Did your voice sound different than when you spoke the negative thought? Again, pay attention to your energy and compare the two.

Successful thinking, like a giant magnet, draws successful people and circumstances together into your life. It's *Thought – Action – Result*. In the tangible world, you solve thoughts of hunger by eating something. When you have thoughts of weariness, you sleep and wake up refreshed. You eliminate thoughts of being cold by turning on the heat, and you are warmed. It is exactly the same in the intangible.

Example 1

Thought: "I can't set a goal to be debt-free because I've been in debt all my life and owe just too much money. I could never earn enough money to repay what I owe."

Action: This person has attracted lack and debt. He/she takes no action to change this pattern.

Result: This person remains in financial distress.

Example 2

Thought: "I'm setting a goal to get rid of my dependency on overeating, but I'm afraid I will get hungry."

Action: This person starts a healthier eating program but, before long, is feeling hungry all the time and quits.

Result: This person gains even more weight.

Example 3

Thought: "I will have my loan with the bank paid back by June."

Action: This person starts putting into place the things needed to increase their income.

Result: This person becomes more creative and lives in a proactive mode, meeting people who are in a position to help.

> An unexpected check appears in the mail, and he/she receives some financial advice they had never heard before. Their loan is paid back by June.

Read again just the three example thoughts. Do you see the difference between the first two and the third?

Look at your life, choose an example of *Thought – Action – Result,* and then write it below.

____

____

____

____

____

If it is a positive experience, write what you did that made it work. If it is a negative experience, write what you could have changed to make it a positive outcome.

____

____

____

____

Your goal choice and decision is based on your feelings that it is a right goal for you. It has either found you, or you thought about a goal and experienced a sense of "Yes!" You had a feeling of excitement, without hesitation, and a desire to commit to getting started. The right brain is at work in all its glory! There is a bit of left brain involved when it comes to deciding on the right wording for your goal, but when that is accomplished, it's time to hand control back to the right brain. Do not try to analyze how you are going to do it—you could be arrested for goal murder. Your right brain is so creative that it will have the ways and means for you to reach your goal, giving you pop-ups right in your eyes. Once these systems are solidified, you can visit your left brain for a while to do some planning and structure.

Always remember that negative thoughts produce negative results, and positive thoughts produce positive results. If you make even a one-degree change in your normal thinking pattern, within one month you will be in a whole new place. You will have shifted.

Either you give your thoughts direction or the outside world will. Simply replace thoughts of fear with thoughts of courage, thoughts of illness with thoughts of health, thoughts of hate with thoughts of love.

The Law of Thinking is all about using your conscious mind, not just about a mind being busy, but really using it to produce desired results. We are progressive beings and if we are not 'thinking,' we are not growing, and that's why so many of us get stuck.

As already stated, you are an Essence, and that Essence flows through you from a Divine Source. That Divine Source is what creates the desire in you to be, to do, and to have more. Remember, we are progressive beings. Your right brain is creative and steps in at this point, morphing your desires into thoughts which in turn become ideas. Directed toward a purpose, those thoughts and ideas become your goals. By reaching your goals, you grow, and that is what your Essence wants for you. That is the goal of your goals, to grow into all that you are and can possibly be, and then you have true happiness.

Take a moment to determine how you will change the way you think, and then write it down.

____

____

____

____

____

The Law of Compensation

Are you satisfied with what you are receiving in life? In your relationships, your career, your health, your spirituality, your physical environment, your family. If you answered yes to most of these, you are very rare. Most people are dissatisfied and don't feel they are fairly rewarded for their efforts.

What do you think of yourself? Describe the kind of person you really truly think you are.

____

____

____

____

What do you think you have a right to in life? Be honest.

____

____

____

____

What do you long for that you don't have? Go deep.

____

____

____

____

If, in your answer to the first question, you used any negative words about your appearance, your behavior, or your lifestyle, you are normal. If the answers to the second question were not all the very best there is this world can offer, you are normal. If the answer to the third question was that you feel mad or sad that you don't have something, you are normal.

Do you want to remain normal?

I'm guessing you don't. So how do you fix this? Let's start by looking around you.

What condition is your home in?

____

____

____

____

What condition is your car in, inside and out?

____

____

____

____

How do you usually dress?

____

____

____

____

Closets, drawers, garage – what condition are they in?

____

____

____

____

What bad habits do you have, e.g., tardiness, smoking, illicit drug use, overeating, over-anything, abusing or allowing abuse?

____

____

____

____

Read your answers over very carefully. Then ask yourself, "Have I been excruciatingly truthful?" If not, make corrections. This will be of no use to you if you pull the wool over your own eyes.

Here is an irrefutable truth. When you look at a person's surroundings and how that person treats himself/herself and his/her belongings, you have a clear picture into that person's mind. The Law of Compensation delivers to you in exact proportion to your image of yourself. That dang law is just so smart! You cannot fool it, so you may as well work with it rather than against it.

Go back to that thing you long for and don't have. There is one rule that must be met with this desire. It cannot be based on changing someone else's behavior, i.e., I long for (this person) to change the way (he/she does or doesn't) act. You can never change other people; you can only change your reaction to them. You would be better to say, "I long to feel and think differently about how (this person) (does or doesn't) act so that I can have freedom and peace."

There is no limitation on you other than that which you put on yourself. You can change anything you like. You can have anything you want. You are empowered when you take total responsibility for your life, when you take ownership for everything in your life, and when you hold yourself accountable.

From the very moment you do this, your life will shift on such an angle you better find something to hang on to, because the ride is thrilling!

When you keep your surroundings clean, tidy, and orderly, your life will become clean, tidy, and orderly. When you respect your body and lead a healthy lifestyle, you will become healthy, vibrant, and never lack for energy. When you do more than you are paid to do, you will get a better position or find that your business is growing exponentially.

You can live life by default or by design—intelligent design. The Law of Compensation helps those who help themselves. When you become better, you will get better. You must earn what you want or you can't have it. It may appear to you that some people do get things they seemingly don't deserve. First of all, it is not our place to judge. We cannot know the details of another's life and if they haven't earned it, they will lose it. It's always best to leave other's lives up to them; you have enough on your plate with just you.

It is the image you have of yourself that is the core of working with the Law of Compensation. As this image improves by right thinking and right action, things in your life will be right.

One word of caution: sometimes life does not deliver in equal proportion. You may feel that you have worked long enough changing your image of yourself, giving more than what you are paid to do, dressing better, and you even quit smoking! So when is this reward coming anyway? Are you doing these things in order to be rewarded or are you doing these things in order to grow larger and to be a better and happier human being? When we receive more reward than we have earned, do we complain? There is a divine, perfect order working in the background, it is not for you to put deadlines on it, it is for you to trust in it. The law is immutable; it always works.

I learned something a number of years ago that I found so profound that I adopted it as my philosophy of life, "Create value in all things." And I do.

In what ways will you make changes in the image you hold of yourself from this moment on?

____

____

____

____

Keeping the Law of Compensation in mind and working with it as you choose and travel toward your goals will go a long way to ensuring your choice of goals are the right choices.

The Law of Forgiveness

"There is a power within you that is bigger than the hurt you feel."
— Bob Proctor

Forgiveness is a shift in your perception of something that is blocking your awareness of love's presence. That sentence is paraphrased from *A Course in Miracles* and could well be the most powerful sentence in this entire book.

It is painful, the great number of people who hold grudges, make assumptions, and otherwise poison their lives by putting blame on others. They hold on to it and talk about it and think about it almost constantly, as if it were a life preserver and the only thing keeping them from drowning. Each time they talk about it or think about it, their negative emotional energy mixes in, and they build that block bigger and stronger while love's presence becomes even more remote.

Those who are stuck in their inability to forgive don't realize that their thoughts and emotions directed toward the target person or circumstances of their turmoil are not hurt or affected by it. The only one hurt and affected is the one unable to forgive. Energy returns to its original source. All that negativity courses through their body and psyche spreading disease (that is, *dis*-ease) and affects everything they do in life. While the target of their inability to forgive, usually unaware of the misery aimed at them, they are simply blithely going about life. To the unforgiver, I often shock them by saying, "That person is living rent-free in your head, and it's time to evict them."

The vast majority of hurt you feel was not meant by the person being blamed. Most often it is a misunderstanding, and if the person being blamed was aware of your feelings—your true feelings of pain, not a verbal onslaught—that person would in most cases feel bad and want to make things better. Proper communication is what is missing in these circumstances.

Now, if someone deliberately planned and premeditated an act to purposely cause you hurt, they have violated one of the Universal Laws and, being immutable, the law will react.

- Action – Reaction
- Reap – Sow
- Give – Receive

However you understand it, the law works.

So that leaves the unforgiver with a choice. It's not about what someone did to you or what you imagine they did to you, it is about how you react.

How does one forgive? Well, let's first make one thing very clear: forgiveness is not condoning the other party's action.

It is not OK that someone lied about you.

It is not OK that someone stole from you.

It is not OK that someone cheated you out of what was yours.

It is not OK that your father or mother left you as a child.

It is not OK that you were abused as a child.

It is not OK that someone murdered your loved one.

It is not about you having to tell them, "It's OK, I understand." In fact, the other party isn't even in on this. They remain oblivious. The answer is very simple.

You let go.

If you are in a tug of war using a huge thick rope with you on one end and someone else on the other and you let go, who falls on their derrière in the muck? Doesn't it feel good to let go? Do this enough times and you won't even pick up the other end of that rope!

The Buddhists say that being unforgiving is like holding a hot red coal in your hand and intending to throw it at the other person. Who gets burned? Stop the pain and drop it. Just let it go.

Unforgivingness and resentment are like eating arsenic every day, intending for the other person to die. Who dies? Stop poisoning yourself. Let it go.

Letting go is for you. With it, you release the thoughts and feelings of resentment, one of the most damaging emotions there is. When you forgive and let go, you are the recipient of the good. Your mind is freed to think beneficial and beautiful thoughts again, and you can get back to living your life.

Looking at the other side of this door to forgiveness, one person we most often need to forgive is the one looking back at you in the mirror. This involves another dangerous emotion: guilt. In looking at your past behaviors and feeling a horrendous burden of guilt, you can throw off the hair shirt by realizing you likely did the best you knew with the knowledge you had. It's a shift in your perception that can remove your block to love's presence. As discussed in the previous chapter, perhaps what you think you did that is causing this guilt was not actually what you did, but someone's interpretation of what you did that you adopted as your own due to conditioned belief systems.

I've done this process. I made a choice to let go of resentment. What happened then was wondrous. With the resentment gone, there was an empty space. The Big U loves a vacuum and rushes in to fill it. My perception of the person to whom my resentment was aimed began to change. Little by little, new thoughts were forming, things I had never thought of previously. Not much time passed before I had a completely new perception of this person, and I realized that this person had not caused me to feel resentment. I had, with my own twisted version of this person's actions. The awareness of love returned, and I knew that I did indeed love this person and that this person did indeed love me. This person was my mother. I came to this place of peace and love five years after her passing.

There has been a shift since then, a shift in my own life that I can hardly believe. Beautiful, wonderful things are happening. Things I have wanted to happen for a long time, goals I have been striving for but that had stalled. The doors that have opened, the opportunities that have presented themselves, the people who have come in to my life are all perking in a synergy, propelling me to new heights of fulfillment, peace, joy, and love. I thank my courageous mum, who I didn't fully understand, and my ability to let go and work within the Law of Forgiveness.

Very recently, during the writing of this book, my willingness and ability to forgive was put to the test. At home in Canada, our beloved cat, Sid, slowly developed a bowel condition which required him to receive enemas occasionally as well as medication and diapering. Now, I know what you are thinking, how in the heck do you diaper a cat without suffering the punctures and scratches of 20 claws? The answer is very carefully and with a system.

Sid was a highly evolved cat. He suffered indignities of diapers, enemas, and baths in soapy water in the sink between changes with such aplomb and cool. First, he trusted me implicitly. We had a bond that is very special. Second, he knew we were helping him.

He was making good progress when it came time for us to travel south in our motor home coach to spend the winter in Yuma, Arizona. As soon as we arrived, we checked in with our Arizona veterinarian to bring him up to speed on Sid and on the new addition to the family, Atma.

Two weeks later, we were scheduled to travel in the coach to Las Vegas where I was attending a three-day business event. It became evident that Sid required another enema before we traveled, and we took him to our vet for the procedure. When we went to pick him up later that day, the vet told us he found some scar tissue and felt that if he broke it down it would solve Sid's problem completely and so he had done that instead of the enema.

The morning of leaving for Las Vegas, we stopped in at the clinic for a quick check up. Sid had a slight fever and a bit of swelling where his tail met his body. Antibiotics were prescribed and off we went to Las Vegas to stay in an RV park for a few days. Sid's swelling got worse, and we doubled the antibiotics hoping they would work quicker. A couple of days later, he stopped eating, the swelling was worse, his skin had turned black, and puss was seen. We then rushed him to an after-hours animal emergency hospital where were told he had a vicious infection and he was in shock and would have died that night if we hadn't brought him in.

That night and the next day, he was treated with everything in their arsenal, was stabilized, and then was referred to a veterinary referral hospital for urgent difficult cases. A talented surgeon explained all the alternatives for Sid, and the first thing to do was perform surgery to see if he had enough viable tissue left after the infection to repair his bowel.

During this surgery, the surgeon discovered this was not the case. Sid had less than a 10% chance of healing properly, and even then his chances for any kind of quality life were zero. Our hearts in agony, we made the decision to let him go and rushed to the hospital to be with him. I held him in my arms, his head soaked with my tears, and my hubby put his hand on Sid's heart as the doctor performed the euthanasia. He was my special sweet boy, and I cried for two days.

The vets at both Las Vegas hospitals agreed with our suspicion that the procedure the vet in Yuma performed one week previously had caused a tear in Sid's bowel, thus the infection, the peritonitis, and so on. The vet to whom we had entrusted our beloved pet caused his death.

We allowed ourselves to grieve, received his ashes, and helped Sid's brother to adjust to life without him over the next few weeks. We then visited our Yuma vet to talk with him, not knowing what his reaction would be. We calmly presented what had happened with Sid in Las Vegas very factually in a report we prepared for him. We stated that we had no intentions to litigate, because it was not in the spirit of Sid as he would have been the first to forgive. We know this vet did not intentionally harm Sid, that he made a mistake with sad consequences, and that all we asked is that he compensated us for the expenses of Sid's Las Vegas care, which amounted to a few thousand dollars.

This doctor did not make excuses, did not deny his culpability, expressed his very sincere remorse, thanked us several times for coming to see him, and told us we would be hearing from him. A few days later, we received his check in the mail covering all the expenses and again a note of sincere apologies.

I know that this doctor's character, ethics, and values are unusual when it comes to the majority of people when facing up to something they have done to hurt or harm another. In my estimation, this is worth many Buddha points!

It did not change the fact that we had lost our beautiful Sid in a horrible manner, that he suffered in the process, and that it need not have happened. However, the doctor is human, he made a mistake, and we all make mistakes. It is what we do after our mistakes that truly count.

How do you forgive someone who is responsible for the death of someone you love?

1. Put yourself in their shoes to get a different perspective to add to your own.

2. Ask yourself, would my loved one want me to remain in pain indefinitely?

3. Do nothing motivated by anger or any other negative emotion.

4. If you decide to communicate with the person, accept beforehand whatever reaction they may have and know that

they own it and not you. You go in with no preconceived or scripted outcome. It is part of your healing to speak your truth as long as it is done with respect, no matter what the other person has done or how they take it.

5. Examine your own life purpose, values, and philosophy. They can bring you peace.

One of my top five values is 'inner peace.' I could not have that if I harbored hatred, resentment, a 'poor me' attitude, or anger. My philosophy is to create value in all things, which was difficult in this instance. Here's what helped. Just as I know we have a purpose in being on this planet, so do all living things, including Sid. If part of his purpose was to provide a learning experience for the vet, for us, and for anyone hearing his story, then who am I not to accept that?

Events occur the way they do for reasons. No amount of 'what if' will change them; you can only torture yourself. Previously in this book, we talked of the enormous power your thoughts have with the energy they produce. It comes down to, what do you want? To tear yourself down or build yourself up? To be happy or miserable? To be sick or well? You hold the power.

In the realm of reaching your goals, if you are still hanging on to that rope in a tug of war, you need to let it go.

Whom do you need to forgive?

____

____

What are you going to do?

This has been a difficult chapter for me to write because I decided to examine only three of the many Laws of the Universe. And that was the difficulty. I wanted to choose three that I felt had the most effect on choosing and attaining goals. They all have a tremendous effect! But I made my choices and, in the end, am pleased with those.

I ask you to keep in mind that I have only skimmed the vast knowledge available on the Laws of the Universe. There is much more and could be a book all by itself. In fact, many have already been written.

Remember to flow with the current, to work with the laws, such as the Law of Thinking, the Law of Compensation, and the Law of Forgiveness and all the Universal Laws. In doing so, you are 'building it' so 'they will come.'

Resources

Working With the Law, Raymond Holliwel

As a Man Thinketh, James Allen

Chapter Seven

Can You Believe It?

Believe: The dictionary defines 'believe' as to accept as true. Lynn's Dictionary defines it as consider the 'Source.'

"Life is as good as your relationship with yourself."
— Unknown

If you have been aware of setting goals but have never consciously gone Goaling up to now, why do you think that is? Write your answer.

____

____

____

There are some popular justifications in response to this question. The most common are:

- I don't set goals.
- I tried it once, and it doesn't work for me.
- I can't overcome my procrastination.
- I'm afraid to because if I didn't reach them, people will think I'm a failure.
- I get distracted.
- I never know if a goal is right for me.
- I don't know the steps to follow.

What strikes you about these reasons? There is a commonality. Let's take them one at a time.

I don't set goals. Yes, you do. Remember Chapter One? You think, therefore you set goals. When you think in negativity and fear, you attract things that are negative and things you fear. Let's say you have a fear of being broke. You often find yourself thinking, "I don't want to be broke." Did you know that the Big U cannot recognize words of negativity, such as don't, can't, won't, not? All it hears is, "I want to be broke." Guess what? You're broke! We know from Chapter One that we are all goal setters because we attract to our lives what we think about. We will find what we are looking for in life, good or bad. The Laws of the Universe work all of the time, and no one is exempt.

I tried it once, and it doesn't work for me. This sounds like a conscious effort, and that's good. This person just didn't have the right information and gave up after a first try. Perseverance is a good and necessary quality for Goaling.

I can't overcome my procrastination. There's that word can't again. All she has to do is drop the -t. Goals come in cans, not can'ts.

I'm afraid to because if I didn't reach them, people will think I'm a failure. This person gets kudos for honesty. People? People! Why would you carry a crowd of people in your head, all living there rent-free? Who cares what other people think of you? People who pass judgment on others are really coming from a perspective of low self-esteem. They don't like what they see in the mirror and think that by criticizing others, they may feel better about themselves. The more they put others down, the more company they have on their level. They aren't conscious of this, but it's the premise behind this behavior. They are coming from Ego, which judges out of fear, not Spirit, which gives out of love. And besides, no one has to know or has any business knowing anything about your goals. What this person is really saying is that he/she would consider himself/herself a failure, and that is sad.

I get distracted. This is an excuse, not a reason. The reason is deeper, and this person allows distraction in order to not acknowledge a festering fear. It's procrastination in disguise.

I never know if a goal is right for me. Too much head work and not enough heart work. We will know if a goal is right if we feel it is right. This person needs some practice and guidance in learning how to recognize feelings. Of course, everyone knows how to recognize negative emotions, such as anger, disappointment, and sadness, but the positive ones seem to need more fine tuning.

I don't know the steps to follow. So? Go find out.

All flippancy aside, as asked above, what strikes you about these reasons? Take a moment to think about it, and then write it down.

____

____

____

____

Here's what strikes me. It's their belief system.

Did you know that we are born with only two fears? Fear of falling and fear of loud noises.

So where did the rest of our fears come from? Programming.

Our wonderful little impressive minds were taught beliefs by others. And where did they get their beliefs? Same place, from others. And so on and so on.

As an example of how ridiculous this is, think back to the era of Christopher Columbus. Most people said the world was flat and everyone believed it. But not Ol' Chris. He looked around him, saw the movement of the sun, moon, tides, seasons, and developed his own belief system from facts. He believed so strongly that he set out to prove it. He convinced Queen Isabella I to believe it enough so that she sprung for the expense. We all know the result of Chris' journey. A wonderful example of a person thinking for themselves.

But as little kids, we are often squashed when we question things. Eventually we stop questioning. Thinking that they are protecting us, our parents and care givers use the words 'no' and 'don't' more often than any others.

No, don't touch that pot, you'll get burned. Don't cross the street, you'll get hit by a car. Don't eat too much, you'll get a stomach ache and have bad dreams. No, you can't have a drink now, you'll wet the bed.

And then there is the word 'careful.'

Be careful, you might trip and fall. Be careful, there might be poison ivy over there.

They try to keep us safe and unknowingly use fear tactics that cause us to become fearful about so much, especially trying new things. Everything about us has been conditioned so deeply inside us that we can't recognize conditioning for what it is.

As infants, we are the most authentic we will ever be in our lives. We let it be known when we are hungry, uncomfortable, and need a diaper change. Our parents coo and smile at us, play patty cake with us, sing to us, play choo-choo train with a spoonful of smashed green goo that was once peas, and care for our every need. But at a certain stage, we have to become socialized and start fitting in, which is when the conditioning begins. Be an observer of yourself when you are around children, and you will hear the messages you received as a child.

We go to school and face a whole new army of influence from teachers, older students, and our peers. We attend our church, temple, or mosque and belief systems keep piling up. Now we reach the age when it is time to leave the nest and fly on our own. That's when our real education begins. If we are fortunate, we will find ourselves with a skilled mentor to teach us the truths of the Universe, guide us, and allow us to form our own beliefs. Often, what we have to do first is unlearn some of the beliefs that are just not working. And that can be a lifetime for some.

So where does that leave us goalers? Just reading what I have written can start the process of setting you free. Until we acknowledge something, we cannot change it. Now you know your belief systems were taught to you at a vulnerable stage in your life. Of course, not all belief systems are negative. Some of us were fortunate to be in the presence of enlightened adults and parents. This is in no way a criticism of parents who just didn't know better. I was one of them! I and all other parents were also taught our belief systems, and so it goes from one generation to the next. Placing blame or judgment on someone else leaves you powerless to change your experience. Taking responsibility (the ability to respond) for your beliefs and judgments gives you the power to change them. Now that you know this, you can choose which belief systems are not serving you well and begin the unraveling process. Goaling requires the absence of fear.

How, you ask? The process began for me when I stumbled upon a mentor who did seminars called "Balanced Successful Living." His name was Val van deWal, and he had a personal story that could bring tears to your eyes. He was a rotund fellow with a booming voice, wore his gray hair in a Dutch boy cut, smoked cigars, loved to laugh and make others laugh, and wore the most delicious smelling cologne.

Members of my family (because I cajoled, begged, and dragged them) and I attended numerous seminars of Val's over the following years. He unlocked the door to a magical new world we didn't know existed, as if we just woke up one day and our lives went from plodding down the same old familiar road to nowhere to taking an abrupt turn in a new direction that was full of exciting new discoveries, ah-ha moments, fun, motivation, and understanding. There is no doubt in my mind that I was guided to Val. It was at a do-or-die moment in my life, and I was lost. It was as if he took me by the shoulders, turned me in the right direction, gave me a little boot in the butt, and told me, "Go, learn, teach, learn more, teach more. You have much to do."

I shudder to think where my life would have gone without that man. I've had many teachers since then in the guise of books, CDs and DVDs, live events, and some everyday people, and I will always be grateful to Val for opening me up to receive all these treasures and, in turn, help others.

I love one of the stories he used to tell about belief systems. He would often be invited over to the home of a friend to enjoy dinner with him and his family. This one time, he noticed his friend's wife preparing a roast for the oven. Everything she was doing was fascinating and certainly set in motion the anticipation for a delicious meal. She rubbed a savory smelling herb combination on the meat, inserted slivers of garlic in tiny slits on the surface, and prepared onions to caramelize in the roasting pan as the succulent meat browned and crisped. And then she did something puzzling to him. She sliced each end off of the roast before she put it in the pan. With a slight frown he asked, "Why did you just slice off the ends of the roast?" To which she replied, "That's the way my mother taught me." For clarity, Val said, "But I still don't see why." Looking at him as if he was a bit dense she said, "Well, so it will fit in the pan."

Val looked at the pan with the roast in it, looked at his hostess, back to the pan, and then asked, "Do you see what I see?"

You've probably figured out that there was more than enough room in the pan for the whole roast, but this cook had watched her mother cut the ends off her roasts before putting them in the oven time after time after time. She had an unconscious belief system that in order to cook a good roast just like her mother did, she had to cut the ends off it. But when she thought about it consciously, she realized her mother probably did have a small roasting pan and had to trim the roast to fit, but it was ridiculous for our cook to do so.

That is a rather comical and harmless belief system, but it does illustrate just how easily we can be conditioned.

Doing the unraveling of the belief systems that harm your life and do not serve you is not something you should do on your own. Help can range from that of a therapist to a mentor to a knowledgeable friend. It is one reason life coaching has become so popular.

You have that one person who is there just for you. Her primary focus is you. She is a listener (how many people really *listen* to you?), a supporter with only your interests in mind, a cheerleader, a shoulder should you need one, a wise advisor, a guide, and someone who coaches out of you things you did not know were in there. The results are extraordinary. Oh, and she is not afraid to give you a toe to the tush now and then provided she has permission.

Life coaches choose a niche of practice. Mine is bringing people together with what they are longing for through fail-safe Goaling that works and I have been setting and achieving goals all my life. Coaches are relatively new on the horizon, but their popularity and the need for them is growing immensely.

I must tell you the story of an unusual man. Raised in Vancouver, Canada, in a home with two sisters, a mother, and a grandmother during the Great Depression, he made his escape from this harem as soon as he could, at the age of 16. I can understand why, because his grandmother was a tyrant, his mother a university-educated woman who wanted him to follow in her footsteps, one sister also well educated but of a delicate emotional nature, the other a snob, and with no male role model, he wanted out.

He headed north where few women would likely venture, to Whitehorse in the Yukon Territories, where he spent many years indulging in pastimes like panning for gold. Some of his activities included welding on the Alaska pipeline with the U.S. Army during World War II. He was unable to join the Canadian Forces because of one deaf ear.

He read voraciously and thus, in a manner of speaking, continued his education. However, having not heard many of the more complicated words spoken by anyone; he would often mispronounce them throughout the rest of his life. I remember hearing him say, "Pa-*lat*-able (emphasis on the middle syllable) instead of palatable. When he was corrected, he would say, "It wasn't often a bearded, horseback riding, rifle toting, he-man in need of a bath for two months would shovel a spoonful of canned beans from a tin plate to his hungry mouth, close his eyes in rapture, and expound, 'Such an exquisitely palatable dinner, my friends!'"

During one of his sojourns out of the north and back to Vancouver for a couple of months, he met a lady at a YMCA dance and was instantly and totally smitten. This lovely lady was also the mother of a little four-year-old girl with whom he became even more smitten. The three of them married in 1947, and two more children rounded out the family. The north didn't see him again for many, many years.

The wanderlust remained in his heart for the next three decades, but he became a loving family man and only continued his traveling with continued reading of adventure authors, such as Louis L'Amour. Several times over those years, he could be heard saying, "One day, I'm going to ride a bicycle across Canada. It's the only way to really see the country." At the age of 65, he figured it was now or never and told his wife that's what he was going to do the following summer.

And he did.

It was April that year when he dipped the front wheel of his bike into the freezing Pacific Ocean in Victoria, hopped aboard, and off he went. In his panniers, he carried a pup tent, a couple of changes of clothing, tools for bike repairs, a can of WD-40, duct tape, and the odds and sods of whatever a man of 65 feels he needs.

For the most part his route was Trans-Canada Highway 1. Anyone traveling this highway regularly, like truckers or Greyhound buses, got to know he was out there. C.B. radios would sputter to life, and one would hear, "Wonder where Cross Canada Grandpa is today. Let us know if you see him." Later, you would hear, "Just spotted Cross Canada Grandpa about X miles east of (wherever), so keep an eye out for him if you're in the area." The drivers would honk their air horns and wave to let him know they were looking out for him. His loved ones had made certain people know what he was up to by having stitched red lettered words on the back of his white nylon jacket which read, "Cross Canada Grandpa."

Comfortable talking to anyone for any amount of time, he would often lose track of time, much to the dismay of his wife when he was expected home, but during his cross-country sojourn, this characteristic got him invited to many homes where he was served wonderful, home-cooked meals and even offered a real bed for the night. Alternate plans were to sleep in his pup tent or a hostel if he found one.

Then came the day in early August when he reached St. John, Newfoundland, and dipped his front wheel in the equally freezing Atlantic Ocean. He had made a promise to his wife that he would be back home before their wedding anniversary on August 8. After boarding a plane and getting home in a few hours, as opposed to a few months via bicycle, he did just that.

The next few months were spent regaling one and all with stories accumulated along his journey, especially his favorite. Hands-down, the very best treatment for hemorrhoids caused by the months of sitting while pedaling was WD-40!

However, he was far from through.

Several years later, in his early 70s, the pull of the north was so strong it could no longer be ignored. He wanted to go to Whitehorse, Yukon, both to revisit those times of his youth and to see how much things had changed since then.

Now, it just so happened, the newly built senior center in his city was struggling to make its mortgage payments and a call for help had been sent out to its members. That was all he needed. He told the board he was going to cycle to Whitehorse and back and would take pledges from the citizens of the city to make per-mile donations.

Preparations went quickly, including plenty of media coverage, and the pledges came pouring in. Among great fanfare, he pushed off on a spring day full of sunshine and promise.

But it was not to be. Traveling northward in British Columbia is nothing like traveling eastward in southern Canada. The weather was against him. He couldn't carry enough warm, dry clothing, he found himself constantly wet from spring rains, and his pup tent arrangement wasn't especially conducive to a warm bath and electric clothes dryer. He became very ill with pneumonia and had to return home by bus.

Word reached the media and the coverage touched the heart of a local car dealership owner who offered the loan of a camperized van to accompany him if he could find a driver and wanted to make another attempt. Guess who ended up being the driver? His wife, of course.

Off he set again, this time with the knowledge that he had a dry warm place to sleep each night and a hot meal and the company of his wife. She sometimes followed the bicycle in the van and sometimes drove a ways up ahead where she would then wait for him to catch up. Both agreed this could never have been done without the aid of the vehicle, especially when the overzealous driver of a truck side-swiped him with his right rear view mirror and knocked him off his bike. Thanks to his wife and the van, he was able to reach a hospital where a grapefruit-sized swelling on his hip ended up being a bleeding bruise, but no bones had been broken. It took weeks for the swelling to subside, but he was back on the bike after a couple of days. And no, the driver of the truck did not stop.

After many weeks, he and his wife had made it to Whitehorse and were given the keys to the city, wined, dined, and entertained. Then, they turned around and made the return trip. He raised thousands of dollars for the senior's center, had once again thrilled his city with his adventures, and had—this time—been able to share it with the woman he loved.

Was this man a goal setter? Without doubt. Did he quit when the going got tough? No, he met adversities head on. Both trips included many times when he wanted to quit, when the conditions became almost unbearable. But even without the van, he was ready to set out again to Whitehorse after he got well.

What kind of purpose, passion, and belief systems do you think he had? Well, we can't know for certain, but undoubtedly they were powerful. Did he allow his upbringing and early adulthood to be excuses for poor character or behavior, his having an absentee father a reason to be pitied? He chose to have all these circumstances make him a better man, and that he was.

His name was Don, but I call him Dad. You see, I was the little four-year-old girl, and my mother was the lady with whom he had became smitten at the YMCA dance.

OK, back to our own belief systems.

Many of the belief systems we hold that don't serve us well have to do with emotional behavior as a child. Remember how we often got the directive, "Behave yourself," and we knew automatically what that meant.

List some ways you were told *not* to behave.

____

____

____

____

____

____

____

____

____

Perhaps you wrote some of these:

- Big boys don't cry.
- Don't raise your voice.
- Settle down.
- Don't you look at me like that.

- Pouting will spoil your pretty face.
- Don't you dare walk away from me when I'm talking to you.
- That's no way to behave at the table.
- Perk up, things can't be that bad.
- Stop skipping and walk like a lady.
- Don't be silly. There is nothing under the bed.
- You're a big girl now. You can stay by yourself for a couple of hours.
- It's not nice to say things like that about someone else.
- Who do you think you are, young man?
- You should be grateful.

All of the above tell us that whatever we are feeling should not be expressed. Sadness, anger, playfulness, happiness, fear, loneliness, guilt, excitement, worry, power, and the list goes on.

It may be done inappropriately, and the people who have authority over us as children are almost always unaware of the damage they are causing. But the reason behind their behavior is to mold us with what they feel is acceptable behavior, so we will fit in, not be ridiculed, and thus not be hurt. Again, it is done to protect us. How ironic it is that the protection we really need is from this kind of control.

Rather than learning how to behave appropriately, this is what we learned:

- Emotions are childish. (Adults control their emotions.)
- Only adults can have power. (Anger is powerful.)
- Emotions are dangerous. (They lead to feelings and bad behavior.)

A child's survival depends on the good will of the parent or guardian. The child instinctively knows this. So the child makes a decision to become perfect so that the parent will be happy. Then, if the parent still shows signs of unhappiness for any reason, the child feels they are to blame. That's one heck of a responsibility for a child to take on.

Emotion is energy moving through the body, and it's such an individual process. If we depress even one emotion we think is unacceptable, before long we will feel the need to depress all emotions. When that energy gets blocked, we label it depression. Isn't it true that we are in an epidemic of depression diagnoses? There is nothing sadder than a feeling creature not attempting to feel. In adulthood, there are two emotions we allow: anger for men and sadness for women. Isn't it also the case that women are diagnosed with depression at a much higher rate than men? And isn't it so that men have a much higher rate of heart disease at a younger age?

Let's look at where you feel emotion in your body. Think of a recent time when you experienced a disruptive emotion, especially if it was one you tried to depress. Scan your body, top to bottom, with your eyes closed. Now revisit those areas and check off on the list where you felt the emotion.

Top of head ______________

Temples, forehead, and eyes ______________

Jaw ______________

Throat ______________

Back of neck	____________
Shoulders	____________
Upper chest	____________
Shoulder blades	____________
Heart	____________
Solar plexus	____________
Middle back	____________
Stomach	____________
Abdomen	____________
Lower back	____________
Legs and feet	____________

Your next step is to remain aware of your body the next time you find yourself upset. This is the hard part when you begin your healing, remembering to be aware. It will take some practice. What you *want* to do is just react as you always have. What you *must* do is take the knowledge you have just learned and apply it when you are in the midst of emotion. Not easy, but you can do it, and you must do it if you want to progress. Emotions are used a lot in the Goaling process, so let's make certain you can open up to feelings and know the truth of what they are.

OK, you are feeling angry at your teenager. Walk away. Yes, you must walk away. Now walk, run, scream into a pillow, beat the pillow with a bat, dance, sing, turn cartwheels, whatever you physically need to do to release that emotional energy. You must do this! When you feel you have released as much as you need to, stop and breathe deeply. As you breathe, visualize the divine energy entering through the top of your head and traveling to the very spot where you normally feel emotion in your body according to the exercise you did above. Sense that energy spinning and gradually slowing as you relax. When the energy stops spinning, it begins to melt into your tissue, totally relaxing as you breathe. You think of yourself as blending into your surroundings to a point where your mind can begin to think rationally and accordingly with your new knowledge. You will then know that it was your past conditioning that caused you to react as you have been, and you can make a decision to act differently.

After some practice, you will be able to be proactive rather than reactive. You return to your teenager and sit opposite each other with your knees touching. Looking into their eyes, explain how you feel without blaming them. Talk about how you were conditioned, if you are comfortable with it, and then just leave it at that. Tell your teenager you just wanted them to be aware of how you felt and that if they have any questions, just to ask. Then, leave it alone. Tell them you love them, and go and make a cup of something soothing. You will be absolutely amazed at how much more at peace you feel by just having someone listen to you express your feelings.

Here's a story of a teenage girl who felt entitled to go out with her friends one evening. Her parents told her she could not go. Normally, she tried hard to be a good rule follower, but she felt she was not a child anymore, so she went out anyway. When she arrived home, it was to face the grim looks on her parent's faces. She was in the process of learning how to drive a car at the time, and her parents told her to hand over her learner's license. Her punishment was to have the privilege of driving a car taken away. There was no time limit put on it, and she did not learn to drive until she left home some years later.

Did her punishment teach her not to go out when her parents told her not to? Not likely. Instead, and even though she had always tried to be such a good rule-follower but in a fit of independence deliberately broke a rule this one time, she felt she had lost the love, praise, and acceptance of her parents. The punishment went on indefinitely and, therefore, so did the disapproval. The matter had never been closed and she had never had the love and approval of her parents reaffirmed. Now, she must exercise even more control over herself because one mistake can last forever. And so she must never make a mistake again if she is ever to be loved.

This, like previous mistakes, as is always the case, no doubt caused her to repeat her childhood conditioning when she became an adult. Such is the same for us all. It is the way we survived as children, the only way we knew how. As adults, therefore, we simply set ourselves up to project the same situations we were in as children. We didn't meet with approval as children, and because we feel we failed as children, we don't meet our own approval as adults. We, the grown-up, look at the child within and can't love or approve of her because adults, of whom she is now one, are not meant to love and approve of her. Our craving for love and approval always comes from our inner child.

Undoubtedly, this girl carried a belief that when confronted by anyone in authority over her, she must have done something to feel guilty, she must have done something wrong even though she didn't know what it was. After all, the person in authority carried the same role as parents and, therefore, couldn't be wrong or questioned. Even though she wasn't speeding, if she saw a police car, she would slow down. If accused of something, even if she had never considered it a mistake, she would automatically accept the accuser as being right and beat herself up with guilt. From this comes an inability to trust in her decision-making and a fear of being wrong.

This is only one example of the carryover from childhood to adulthood. We all have our own stories.

The good news is that we can learn to experience our emotions joyfully and appropriately. First, we need to find the blockages and then feed them a little meal of TNT to blow them up. Imagine feeling free and full of joy. These two feelings, freedom and joy, form a team to provide you with an endless supply of courage to find and use that TNT.

All we needed as kids was guidance about how to handle our emotions and not a message that our emotions were bad and should be suppressed. You can still have that compassionate Grown-up who is full of kindness and love that you wished you could have known as a child. Your Grown-up can help you make choices and can guide and support you.

The Grown-up is the adult you. Your compassionate adult will understand the child within you and why she reacts as she does. Your kind adult will explain to you that your emotions are natural, that feelings are very human and real, and that you can funnel them to appropriate behavior. Your loving adult will tell you they love you no matter how you behave, and then will show you how to appropriately express your feelings. Allow the adult you to protect, love, honor, and approve of your child within.

What does this have to do with working with Goaling? Everything.

The conditioning you have brought with you into adulthood is always whispering to you. Unless you are among the few who have enlightened parents, you are carrying baggage. It becomes very heavy when you set out on your goal path and can trip you up. You need to know the voices to listen to and the voices to ignore. Being able to identify childhood conditioning from truth frees you.

You know, it is not Spirit that is undermining you but Ego, in its twisted way, trying to protect you, just as your parents were trying to protect you when they told you not to cross the street instead of showing you how to safely cross the street, teaching you how to move a hot pot so you would not get burned, how to walk on a slippery surface so you didn't fall, be shown what poison ivy looks like so you didn't touch it, have someone listen to your feelings and guide you in appropriately expressing them would have empowered you as a child and changed your life. Being able to identify Sprit from Ego is incredibly satisfying.

But most of us did not have this kind of upbringing, so you love your parents for doing what they knew how to do at the time. They loved you and tried their best. No doubt you have much to be grateful for in your childhood. Keep your focus on the great things that your parents did for you, the fun things and the family traditions they taught you. They are just ordinary people, just like you—but you have the power of choice. You can build on this knowledge and do better. You can parent yourself in a different way. Your goal path can be free of encumbrances from your past now that you have some understanding. One more way to 'build it' so 'they will come.'

Resources

ReCreate Your Life, Marty Lefkoe, http://www.recreateyourlife.com/free/

Recommended: Create an album/journal of all your life's accomplishments to date.

Chapter Eight

What Do You Want?

Do: The dictionary defines 'do' as a verb indicating an action, an activity, or a task. *Lynn's Dictionary* defines it as to get what you want, you must put 'do' between 'you' and your 'what.'

It is certainly very clear at this point that what I wanted was to bring Atma home to Canada with me. This is a story of how tenacity relates to the accomplishment of your goals. In the case of Atma and how she came into my life as one of those goals which found me, the epiphany type, I've learned we are never given a goal we can't achieve. Some may have more potholes or detours in the road than others, and this just means we will learn more and be profoundly grateful when accomplished. The tougher the journey, the more we value the destination.

After several difficult goodbyes, Atma and I are in an airport-bound taxi. As I look at the Kathmandu sights, I realize they are the same as when I arrived, but my perspective is skewed 180 degrees. Everything just looks so normal. I have adjusted, it seems, to Nepal and Third World life. It's not what we are looking at that we see, it is how we perceive it that becomes our truth. After six weeks immersed in the culture and activities of Kathmandu, I have a new perspective.

We check in with Jet Airways, and I am pretty wound up about putting my new baby in the cargo hold. I'm holding up well until I have to put her in the kennel and she begins to cry, whine, and scratch madly at the door. So as not to embarrass myself, I use every ounce of strength I have not to cry, but a couple of tears do leak down my cheeks anyway. Because I have to wait a ridiculous amount of time for a particular person to sign off on an animal passenger, Atma can see me but can't get to me, so the constant crying is breaking my heart.

A wonderful older gentleman whose job it is to transfer the luggage from the desk to the belt notices this, and as I finally walk away toward security, he steps out from behind the desk, looks at me, and nods his head making hand gestures that everything is OK and she will be alright. Bless his heart. Well, I did get upgraded to first class and that helped a little bit.

Next stop, New Delhi. I collect my bags and Atma for the eight-hour layover. She was overjoyed to see me and not the least bit upset. It was wonderful to spend that time together even though I once again was faced with the problem of not being able to get my luggage cart through the washroom doors, so again I had to find someone trustworthy to look after it while Atma and I went to the facilities.

It was never made clear, either going to or returning from Nepal, why I had to pick up my luggage in New Delhi both times instead of checking it through. I was just told this is what I had to do, and I'm such a good little rule follower. But what problems it causes!

It's time to check in with Lufthansa for the trip to Frankfurt, quite a process when you are also checking in a live animal. It was a struggle, but I finally got Atma back in the kennel. To say she was reluctant would be like saying you were a bit uneasy about placing your head in the guillotine. She is quite the little gymnast, what with all four legs going in every direction. And the pitiful crying, whining, and scratching begins in earnest anew. It pulls at my heart especially knowing it will be about 24 hours before I see her again.

I'm now told I need to go to a different desk and make the payment to the airline for the dog and pay the Indian departure tax. The departure tax must be cash but the airline fee can be charged to my credit card. I have no Indian rupees but will use a Visa for the airline and then go to the ATM for cash.

First pothole: There is a hold on my Visa card. I go to the ATM to withdraw all the funds I need.

Second pothole: The ATM card won't work in machine (which never happened in Nepal).

Back to the desk, I'm asking myself, "What am I going to do now?" I only have the one credit card. I think I know the reason for the hold on it. I had not used it since I left home six weeks ago up until I paid for Atma's airfare on Jet Airways in Kathmandu. This would have sent up a red flag as a possibly stolen card. I share this info with the nice gentlemen at the desk and tell them I have to phone the credit card company.

Third pothole: How do I pay for a phone call without a credit card? The call is not free outside of North America. Now I'm getting flustered. Somehow I have to get my hands on 13,000 Indian rupees. A very nice gentleman at the desk gives me his cell phone. Oh boy, angels are everywhere. I dial the number and get a message that they do accept collect calls. Why the blazes don't they put that on the credit card along with the number? But I'm on a roll now, and an agent answers. I'm not only flustered but angry, and those who have seen me flustered and angry always slink away quietly, making very quick exits in the opposite direction.

Fourth pothole: I cannot hear the agent on the phone.

I keep saying, "I can't hear you. Could you please speak up?" All I hear is "I can't do that ma'am," and the rest of his words fade out. I holler, "I'm in New Delhi! My credit card has been cancelled, and I want to know why!" Can't hear his reply. I keep telling him I can't hear him. I try to find a quieter corner where I sit down on the floor, plug my free ear, and keep trying to hear him. No good. Now tears of frustration prick at my eyelids as I listen to Atma nearby perfecting her cry, whine, and scratch routine, and I yell at the agent, "I can't get on that plane until my Visa card works, and I have to get on that plane with my dog!"

I switch the phone to my other ear. Voila! I can hear his modulated, monotone, I-could-care-less voice. Seems I must have touched the volume control during the transfer. He says, "Get them to try the card again." They do, it works! OK, dog fare is paid. Now all I need is cash in rupees to pay the departure tax. I try a different ATM, . . . and it works!

As I trot back to the desk with hot rupees in my hands, I suddenly realize I paid a departure tax in Nepal, so why am I paying a departure tax in India when I never even left the airport? I explain this to the nice gentleman at the desk who looks blankly at me and eventually, after looking around at his colleagues and then back at me, says, "In that case, you don't have to." He then asks when I arrived in New Delhi. Eight hours ago, and I show him my Jet Airways boarding pass. My trip was on two itineraries, and I only showed the one from New Delhi onward when I checked in at the desk in New Delhi. Well, why in heck would I show him the one I had just completed? Sheesh, doesn't he have ESP? Probably the fact that I had all my luggage with me may have confused the issue.

Fifth pothole: Now I have a fistful of rupees I don't need.

Over to the money exchange desk where I am ripped off exchanging rupees to U.S. dollars that had started out as Canadian dollars 15 minutes ago.

They have finally taken Atma out of the check-in area, everything is looked after, and it's 2:00 a.m. As I show my boarding pass at the gate, I realize it is the same young man who checked me in at the desk. He whispers to me, "Atma is onboard. She is doing just fine." Bless his heart, and I tear up again.

I still have a long way to go.

I arrive in Frankfurt eight hours later. My baggage and Atma are checked all the way to Calgary from New Delhi, and I have another eight-hour layover. I pray someone is giving her water and food. There is nowhere to sit in the Frankfurt airport except at the departure gates, and my gate isn't open until one hour before the flight and the gate hasn't been posted yet. I can't sit in any other gate, because they are organized in such a way that you have to show your boarding pass just to get through to the seating area. Lordy, I am intimately familiar with every nook and cranny of Frankfurt airport. The only available seats are in the washroom. I don't drink beer, but I thought to myself, "While in Germany, do as the Germans." So I sit down (phew!) in a bar and have a beer. Is it actually this good or am I just sleep deprived?

Once at the gate, I am paged. A nice lady asks me if I am traveling with a dog, and I confirm that I am. She tells me the dog is here and doing fine. They feel that for the 10-hour flight to Calgary, she needs more room, so they put her in a larger loaner kennel and check my kennel as baggage. Bless their hearts, and more tears.

Sixth pothole: I arrive late to Calgary and miss my connecting flight.

I wrestle my bags on a cart at baggage claim, find my ecstatic dog, who I can't take out of the kennel because we are clearing customs, and everyone in earshot becomes well aware of what Atma thought of that. A simple wave after seeing her rabies vaccination certificate, and we are through. Now to rebook a flight and put Atma and bags on the connections belt. Cry, whine, scratch, tears.

I am now approaching security to get to my gate. A presecurity check is done to ask if I have any liquids or gels. My backpack has my toiletries, and I have forgotten that in Canada one can't carry liquids or gels over 100 ml onboard. All of them have to fit in one miniscule Ziploc bag provided by the airport.

Seventh pothole: My toiletries break the rules. And didn't I just say that I was a good little rule follower?

They were OK through five physical and three X-ray checks in Kathmandu, New Delhi, and Frankfurt—but not in my home country. It is suggested that I check my backpack at the Air Canada desk. So I trot off to do that.

Eighth pothole: It will cost me $100.

Seems I have already checked two bags, which is the allotment for my flight distance, and any additional pieces I have to pay for. I pass. I wonder, will they accept Indian rupees?

Now I'm thinking, I have some small empty bottles in my toiletry bag. Off to the washroom to transfer product into them. It is a messy job trying to get crèmes and lotions through such tiny bottle necks. The tap at the sink spews ice-cold water for five seconds at a time, after which you have to push the button for another five seconds. I have a bottle in each hand, lotion running down the sides, and I have to keep pushing the dang button with my chin as my hands are frozen. OK, done. Everything is 100 ml or less and I get it all to squeeze into that Ziploc bag (with a bit of stretching).

So I head back to presecurity.

Ninth pothole: The nice man who suggested I check-in my backpack has been replaced with a stern-faced woman of large proportion and a badge. Uh-oh.

I proudly show her my Ziploc bag. Puffing out of her chest (the easier to see the badge), she tells me that one of the bottles is too large, it's 200 ml. "But it's half empty and has less than 100 ml of crème in it," I reply. No matter, the bottle can't be larger than 100 ml.

Tenth pothole: She doesn't realize that I have crossed five time zones and been awake for the past 30 hours and am dizzy with jetlag.

Buried deep within my small stature there lays my "Beelzebub Bitch," who I only allow out under certain circumstances. Having dodged nine potholes already, being without sleep for over 30 hours, being worried about my dog, and suffering from jetlagg is such a circumstance.

I argue. What's the difference? It's just air in the bottle with the crème, not liquid or gel, it's crème! This is expensive stuff, and you are going to make me throw it out? It was just fine with Jet Airways in Nepal, Lufthansa in New Delhi, and Air Canada in Frankfurt. Can't you airlines get it together and have some kind of consistency? Why is it OK with Air Canada in Europe but not Air Canada in Canada? Screw it, take the damn thing—and enjoy!

And I stomp off to the X-ray machine. Yeah, I was ripped.

She calls after me, "We don't keep them, ma'am." I toss a bitchy reply over my shoulder, "There's a garbage can right behind you, so throw it in there!"

I was expecting a platoon of security agents to haul me off for 'questioning' or at least to be tasered. Guess I went up to the wire but didn't cross it. Well, I got my blood boiling and my adrenalin glands pumping and, damn, I was feeling better.

Later, I arrive in Kelowna. It's 8:00 p.m. and the sun is still shining. Atma is first off the plane from cargo. I let her out of the kennel and the fastest tongue and tail in the West are a blur. Greg meets us with dog food, water, and bowls. Smart man. She ate, she drank, she ate, and she drank.

One of my bags did not arrive. After what Atma and I had been through the past 36 hours, this is barely a bump in the road, doesn't even qualify as a pothole. I'm home, and it'll turn up.

A very happy puppy, a worn out Mummy (with that Beelzebub woman safely chained back in her cell), a man happy to have his family plus one complete again, and a mound of luggage, minus one, are packed in the car for the short drive back home, sweet home.

Will there be potholes on the way to your goals? Yes. It is clear in the above story what it is I wanted. I wanted it so much that I was ready to risk the potholes. It is this desire, this soul connection to your goal that gets you over and around the stumbling blocks. Added to that is the fact that someone (Atma) other than me would benefit from my goal success. And so the desire is twofold: my desire for Atma and my desire for myself. Such an exquisite, two-sided coin and one of the best kept secrets to Goaling! Remember that it is in the giving that you receive.

It is the plain fact that your goal benefits someone as well as yourself that will keep you from giving up. It is a fact that we will give up on ourselves far quicker than we will give up when someone else will miss out, suffer, or be disappointed.

If I had been going to Nepal just to explore a bit, have a vacation, and meet some interesting people, I doubt very much if I would have remained for six weeks. But young students and monasteries were counting on me, and they needed my knowledge to learn English so they could do better in this world. I could never let them down.

Am I happy Atma and I made the tough journey and arrived at destination, home? Ecstatically so! Would I still have had to dodge potholes if I hadn't brought her with me? Who knows? Probably, but because I succeeded and reached my goal for her and for me, I do not care. Everything I did to rescue her, heal her, feed her, and get her on the aircraft with me to bring her home from halfway around the world disappears from my memory with just one look in those pools of love that are her eyes.

That being said, now it's time for you to know what it is that you really want.

What do you want? Would it surprise you to know that very few people can actually answer that question? Well, they do answer it, but it is usually with, "I don't know." I find that so sad. We often hear people say things that begin with "I wish" or "If only," yet when asked what they want, they don't know.

I think of the story of a young woman who, after just finishing her education, stepped out into the working world as an assistant manager of a department store. It was a good position for a first job and for someone so young. She was very excited about the fact that she was going to be getting a pay check twice a month and finally earning her own income. Freedom at last!

With her first pay check, she took her friends out to dinner to celebrate. It cost more than she had anticipated, and she was left with only enough to see her to her next payday. But what the heck, everyone had a good time. When that day came, she had to pay her parents back for a small loan which she had asked for because the money left over after her celebration dinner hadn't been enough to get her to her next pay day.

She was feeling kind of down because she had less than her whole pay check to last for another two weeks, and rent was coming due, so, looking for a way to forget her problems, she went to the mall to meet some friends. While there, she walked past the window of a shoe store and fell madly in love with a red strappy number that would perfectly match her red and white capri pants. With the new shoes now safely tucked in a shopping bag, she bounced home while deciding where she'd be going out tonight in her new ensemble.

This kind of lifestyle continued for six months after which D.K. (let's call her D.K.) found her credit card maxed out, behind on rent, eating Kraft dinner every day, and an ever increasing loan owed to her parents (we'll discuss the parents another time).

And D.K. did not like her job as an assistant manager, as she had to deal with grumpy employees, had way too much paperwork, and often had to work weekends, not to mention the pay was too low. But now she was stuck, she had debts to pay, and she needed the job.

She was at the home of one of her girlfriend's one day complaining about her lot in life when her girlfriend's father overheard their conversation. He asked D.K., "I've heard you telling Jackie that you don't want some of the things that are happening in your life. D.K., Can you tell us what you do want?" In a split second, D.K. came back with, "More money!"

The girlfriend's father replied, "How much money, D.K.?"

"Enough to pay my parents back, pay off my credit card, catch up on my rent, and fill my fridge with a month's worth of food," D.K. dejectedly answered.

"Those are good things to do, D.K. After you have done those things, what else do you want?" he asked.

"I don't know," answered D.K. with a shrug.

"Where do you see yourself in five years, D.K.?" he pressed.

"I never thought about it," and D.K. shrugged again.

"Hmm," he said, thoughtfully. "Well, do you want to be where you are now?"

"No!" came D.K.'s emphatic response.

"What would you change?" he asked.

"Well, I'd certainly like to be making more money," she said.

"And how would you go about doing that?" he asked.

"I don't know," D.K. repeated.

The father stroked his chin for a moment and then asked, "What do you like to do, D.K.?"

"This'll sound silly, but I like to visit the dogs and cats at the shelter."

"Nothing silly about that," he replied. "Do you like being around animals a lot?"

"Yes, I do, and I'd like to have a dog and a cat when I can afford them," D.K. said.

So the father inquired, "What kind of jobs do you think there are that involve being around animals?"

"Well, I never really thought about it, but there are veterinarians," D.K. offered.

"Yes, anything else?" he added.

D.K. thought a bit more and said, "Probably dog walkers and groomers."

"Uh huh," he responded. "Anything else you can think of?"

"Not really," D.K. answered.

"You said you liked to visit animals at the shelter," the father stated. "What about jobs there?"

"Yeah, I guess there are." D.K. replied. Then she added, "I feel so badly for all those cats and dogs, I wish I could do more for them, especially the ones which have been abused."

"Could you ever see yourself working in a veterinarian clinic, as a dog walker or groomer, or working at a shelter?" he asked.

D.K. thought for minute, then said, "Well, not really. I wouldn't want to watch or do surgery, and I don't think the other jobs pay as much as I would want to make."

"So if you could work with animals, not have to do or watch surgery and get paid a good salary, what kind of job could that be?" the father continued.

Again D.K. thought and eventually said, "I like the idea of rescued animals at the shelter, but I'd like to do more than just look after them until they find homes."

“Ah,” the father said, with a nod of his head, “Maybe you’d like to be involved in the rescuing itself.”

Suddenly D.K. sat straighter, tilted her head to one side with an inquisitive look, and said, “I never thought of that, but it sounds very interesting.”

"Maybe the next time you are visiting the shelter you could ask the people who work there more about the animal rescuers they know,” he suggested.

To which D.K. responded with a deep in-thought tone, “Yeah, I might do that.”

What D.K. didn’t know is her girlfriend’s father was a professional life coach, and life coaches know that everyone has their own solutions inside of them. With the right questioning, a good life coach can gently remove layers of suffocating denial or unknowing and help the client reveal their diamonds.

In D.K.’s case, a seed had been planted in her soil of desire, and she did follow through and ask animal rescuers what they did and how they got their jobs. A couple of years down the road, D.K. proudly wore her uniform as an animal control officer and loved everything that her position entailed. She rescued animals from terrible conditions, spoke to classes of school children, educated pet owners, and finally was guardian to her own cat and dog. Her strong desire for helping animals in need of rescue and her desire to be in a job that filled her passion was more than enough to propel her through the steps to be, do, and have what she wanted. Her goal was realized.

Why is it so important to know what you want? As we now know, you are already a goal setter, consciously or unconsciously, so you might as well be conscious of it. There is a great quote on a T-shirt I have that reads, "You're going to think anyway, so you might as well think big."

But that question, what do you want, still haunts your mind and you might be thinking, "What *do* I want anyway? I must know what I want." Try this.

As in D.K.'s case, start with what you don't want and write that down.

For example, "I don't want to be stuck in this job I don't like."

I hope you made a good, long list.

Listen to the people around you talking to each other. It's OK if they are talking in public, since you're really not eavesdropping. Keep score of how many times you hear negative comments and how many times you hear positive comments. It's a strange thing, but you will usually hear more negativity.

For many, it seems easier to get in touch with what you don't want than what you do want. When people talk about negative things, it is almost always coming from a place of fear. For instance, "I really don't like my job, but I don't have a choice," is really not true when you understand the Universal Laws, but this person may have a fear of change a fear of the unknown, or a fear of failure so he/she remains stuck and can only feel a little bit better by voicing their feelings.

Go back over the list of things you don't want and see if you can name the underlying fear that is hiding beneath each one.

Let's take that list of don't wants and switch them up. All you have to do is list the opposites of the things you don't want. Give it a go.

For example, "I want to have my own business."

____

____

____

____

So what do you think you have here?

You actually have the core of a list of goals—congratulations!

On a scale of 1 to 10 (10 being the greatest desire), go back through your list and rate your desire to have each one in your life.

Now write your list again with the items of greatest desire at the top on down to the ones of lowest desire. You may have assigned the same number to more than one (e.g., two items rated 7, three items rates 5,) and that's OK. Just study those that have the same rating and decide which has just a little bit more desire than another, and then list accordingly.

You are doing great, so let's keep going.

Now, write your top five goals below in order of priority.

1.

2.

3.

4.____

____

5.____

____

Fabulous. You now have your top five goals.

The next step is to do some thinking about how the accomplishment of each goal will benefit something or someone other than you. It will help you if you feel with your heart. Remember, this will be a desire as strong as or stronger than your desire for you to accomplish this goal just for yourself.

1.____

2.____

3.____

4.____

5.____

What could stop you from being, doing, or having the things in your top five goals list? Write as many as you think of.

For example, "I don't know how to start a business."

Let's use the example of "I don't know how to start a business" as one thing that could stop someone. What do you think could be one step this person could take to solve this dilemma? There are probably many ideas depending on the kind of business, and if they haven't decided that yet, this would certainly be that first step.

Now go to your list of reasons that could stop you. Name one step you could take to solve each.

____

____

____

____

____

____

It's a funny thing about the human brain and heart, once you begin with writing just one thing down, you have opened a door and, the next thing you know, you are writing more things down and then more and before you know it the whole process which you may have thought would be difficult has become much easier.

What you have just done is determine your top five goals and by writing steps to solve any reasons that you could be stopped from reaching them, you have actually written your first action steps.

So what do you have in total now?

You have a list of things you don't want in your life.

You have a list of fears underlying these undesirables.

You have a list of the opposites of these undesirables which turn out to be goals.

You have prioritized that list with your heartfelt desires and discovered your top five goals.

You have determined from your heart how each of your top five goals will benefit others.

You have identified anything that could stop you on your goal path and in doing so, you have revealed your first list of action steps.

You have determined goals in this chapter using both the right and left brain. When I ask you to think about what is opposite to things you don't like in your life, you are using mostly your left brain (coming from a mindset). When I ask you to come from the heart, you are using mostly your right brain (coming from a soulset).

Going back a few chapters, remember the epiphanies and the Soul Connections, because this is the manner in which goals will come to you. The work you have just done is not necessary for these goals, because your Divine Source has done it all for you. All you have to do is acknowledge this, believe it, and take the action steps that come to you. These will be your most powerful goals and through them, you will do great things and realize a level of happiness you never thought possible.

You have just done some amazing work in this chapter that asks, "What do you want?" The percentage of the population who does this is in the single digits. I'm standing up and applauding you, so stand up and applaud yourself—go on, no one will know. If you are not alone, go into the bathroom and give yourself silent applause. Because you deserve it.

In the next chapter, you will put strategies in place that will rocket you to the stars.

Chapter Nine

Strategic Action

Action: The dictionary defines 'action' as an energetic activity. *Lynn's Dictionary* defines it as a premium grade Goaling fuel.

So far we have talked about:

- Epiphanies, those goals that miraculously find you and how to recognize them
- Your life purpose, passion, and values and how to align them easily with your goals
- Using your left and right brain to choose exciting motivating goals
- Connecting with Spirit, the magnificent Truth and Source of all enlightenment and your biggest fan

- Universal Laws and how they guarantee goal achievement when you use them as your guides
- Your belief systems and how you can get the ones that don't serve you off your goal radar
- What you want in and for your life

This is the chapter in which we invite the left brain to join our Goaling adventure and put it all together into a strategic plan of action. As they say, here is where the rubber meets the road, the butter meets the bread, and the rock meets the roll. Without a plan of action, your energy will be fragmented and so will your results. You'll find yourself flitting from one thing to another, unfocused, and rarely finishing what you start.

Some chefs are the best in the world due to their creativity, ability to see the finished product in detail, and stay in the moment (both specialties of the right brain). However, they must also be able to follow the recipe, the plan, and if they operate a restaurant, they must figure out how much of each kind of food to have on hand and order from the supplier, which foods can be prepared ahead of time and which can only be done on the spot. They must run their staff and kitchen like clockwork so their patrons are served in a timely manner and their kitchen is kept in a condition that is compliant with food service regulatory laws. This all comes under planning and structure (the forte of the left brain).

The novelist writes stories in which we happily become enthralled for hundreds of pages. The writer has the creativity gene of a fertile imagination and an ability to place themselves into the midst of their adventure and live as one or even as all of their characters. They can write the last chapter before they have written the first chapter and can finish a book before they even have a title. However, no one would publish a book that had the chapters out of order or had no title. The writer must organize the book into segments (chapters), perhaps add a bibliography if necessary, a table of contents, an index, a page of acknowledgments, an introduction and dedication, and have it edited for correct punctuation and grammar. Then there is the process of finding a publisher, and if fortunate enough, deal with the legalities of a contract. The fun of writing and creating are right-brained while everything else is left-brained.

Isn't it always a thrill when fresh flowers are delivered to you? The heavenly fragrance of roses and lilies, the exquisite color combinations, the artistry involved in the choices and arrangements of the flowers are beautifully right-brained. The left brain must look after all the behind-the-scenes aspects of a business. Choosing and ordering stock, hiring staff, operating within the law, planning advertising and promotions, keeping a finger on the financials, and so on.

In most of life's endeavors we need to use our whole brain. The right-brained person has the luxury of being able to outsource or delegate many of the left-brained duties, whereas their creativity cannot be assigned to anyone else. The chef, the writer, and the florist all have something uniquely their own and can enjoy more of their creative passions with wise delegation. The left-brained person has their talents in developing structure and organization, using logic, and their ability to teach others a craft. They have an innate sense of timing, are analytical problem-solvers, and good future planners.

And so it is that we are a combination of both our left and right brains. We are just predominantly more one than the other and to different degrees. If you did the online test I suggested in Chapter Four, you will know your specific balance.

So how do we fit this knowledge in with your Goaling plan of strategic action? I shall use my predominantly left-brained mind to show you how.

A strategic plan is a clear detailed map for you to follow all the way to the attainment of your goals. You can do it yourself, but if you have another clear-thinking person involved to add some diversity, it can be very helpful. Put yourself in a physical environment that is free of phones, computers, and any other potentially disruptive elements. If you have hired a coach, you will likely be on the phone with her.

The Present

This is all about what you have right now that will be the rocket fuel taking you to your goal fulfillment. Write your purpose, your passion, and your top five values. For the sake of ease and so as to not infringe on the privacy of anyone else, I will use myself for examples.

Your purpose:
Who you are and what you are on this earth to do for others.
I am a strong woman leading people to discover their true value.

Your passion:
What you love to do and the drive behind your purpose.

My passion is to learn so that I may teach so that I may learn anew.

Your values:
Your truths that guide your behavior.
Independence, relationships, knowledge, inner peace, achievement.

The Future

Now that you have your rocket fuel, let's go get the rocket. Write your mission and vision.

Your mission: How you live in concert with your purpose and passion and why you are in a specific career or business.

My mission in my business, Clear Goals Coaching, is to encourage people to accomplish their goals by providing specific tools, guidance, and knowledge to lead them to lives of greater independence and abundance. I am in business to fill the need for people to feel optimistic and empowered.

Your vision: This is your statement of ambition, and the sky is the limit! Imagine, in great detail, what you want this goal to look like once achieved. This is a powerful statement that will inspire you every time you read it. (Notice that my vision is stated in the present tense even though this is my vision for the future.)

My business is the brightest spotlight on the Internet for people to learn goal achievement skills. The emphasis is on meaningful results for clients using specialized methods and skills founded in Spirit.

How to Get There

Here is where you list by priority all the goals established in the last chapter, your objectives and your strategies. You are strapped in your space ship, the rocket below rumbling to life, and the countdown begins—and you lift off!

1. **Goals:** List your top five goals as determined in Chapter Eight.
2. **Objectives:** Your objectives support your goals and provide detail on some of the 'how.' As an example, if one of my goals is to land on Google's first page if someone searches for 'coach,' one of my objectives would be to learn more about search engine optimization or hire someone to do it. You could look at objectives as mini goals of action.
3. **Strategies**: Now you need to set some rules and guidelines to help you on your way to the stars in that rocket. You can start by asking yourself the question, "What is getting in the way of me reaching my goals?" As an example, one of my strategies is to remain focused, because I find myself with so many things I need and want to do that I was jumping from one thing to another, fragmenting myself and seldom getting to the end of a task.

The hard part is done. You have the fuel of your purpose, passion, and values. You have the rocket of your mission and your vision and the space ship of your goals, objectives, and strategies. It's time to launch and begin cruising among the stars, for you are one of them, the star of your own life and surely the star in the lives of those you help and serve.

You are also the captain of your own ship, and this is now your job. The captain can't fall asleep at the helm. Just as you would go to a job every day, you must look at reaching your goals as a daily job. Keep your focus on your objectives and your strategies and live them every day.

You already know that once you commit by taking action, the Big U hears you and begins to send opportunities and support systems and assistance your way. Be aware and watch for them.

Stay present, knowing that the value of the past is limited to what it can teach you, the value of the future is limited to planning for it and to be accepting of the fact that you will need to flex when outside influences (potholes) dictate. The only 'time' during which you have any influence or power is the present. Life is but a succession of present moments during which you ask yourself, "What is in my best interests *right now*?"

Your intuition is the voice of your Divine Source, so you must always listen to it and never doubt it. Honor an epiphany—that goose-bumpy feeling in your soul is a goal that has found you!

Stay soul connected from your heart, your mindset becomes your soulset, and you will be guided.

Remember, if you build it, they will come.

Believe in *you*, for you *are* a star!

As a special thank you for purchasing and reading my book,

I have a gift for you.

What has happened to Atma since she arrived in Canada? Would you like to read the rest of her story?

See pictures of Atma when I found her and in the weeks and months following.

Did her hair grow back?

What happened when she was introduced to Lynn's cats?

Did Lynn keep her or find another home for her?

Did she change much?

See pictures of the monklettes, the city of Kathmandu, Atma in hospital, Pokhara from above, the monastery, and so many more!

I have written an extra chapter that answers all the questions above and many more, and it is available on my Web site at:

http://www.inspirationalgoaling.com/freechapter

(and use code 'Atma')

Afterword

The Way I See It

There's good news.

We are experiencing, in the words of Rev. Michael Beckwith, a Birthquake. We are not going to be destroyed. It's as if our Universe has grabbed a megaphone and announced, "Your attention please!" It wants us to receive the gift of a new consciousness. It wants us to wake up and see that the way we are managing this world is not working. We have been Ego-centered and Spirit-starved. And so a shift in energies is happening now.

It will culminate in the year 2012. Please, don't listen to the fear-mongers of a planet exploding into millions of mini planets. This change is not material or physical, it is *energy*. Now fellas, don't take offence, but it is called a Divine Feminine Shift. All men have feminine energies within them and all women have masculine energies within them, yin and yang.

We are evolving from the Age of Information to the Conceptual Age, and the feminine energies of nurture, peace, compassion, collaboration, healing, and understanding are at the forefront.

On the front line are businesses, and we have seen many fall since the Shift began in the summer of 2008, with the resulting domino effect striking millions of people. Businesses with foresight began making changes before this crisis and will survive. What kind of changes, you ask? Good question. They are coming from a place of service, not from a place of grasping. They are moving towards a spirit of cooperation rather than competition. They are connected with making a positive difference in this world. Integrating spirit into business goes a long way to healing and transformation. Not just for business, but for families, schools, sports clubs, volunteer organizations, and so on. Just as the breakdown has its domino effect, our breakthrough has its domino effect—and a new age begins.

The masculine energies of practicality, forging ahead, competition, and forever striving, have done us well in the Ages of Agriculture, Industry, and Information, but now it is time to marry those with the feminine energies so that we achieve balance. The emphasis will be on the feminine energies for a while in order to balance the past over-emphasis on the masculine energies, but the Divine Feminine will bring along the Divine Masculine, and the result will be wonderfully complimentary.

When we speak of masculine and feminine, we speak of energies and not of men and women, for all men and women are of both. When we speak of spirit, we speak of the Divine Essence within each of us, not of religion. We can be both religious and spiritual.

Becoming aware, not fearful, is the order of the day. Fear is not truth. Truth is the Universal Principles and Laws that have been at work since the beginning of time. This is not a time to coast; it is a time to grow. We are on a divine journey to create change. This is an amazing time to be on Earth.

Advantage Media Group is proud to be a part of the Tree Neutral™ program. Tree Neutral offsets the number of trees consumed in the production and printing of this book by taking proactive steps such as planting trees in direct proportion to the number of trees used to print books. To learn more about Tree Neutral, please visit **www.treeneutral.com.** To learn more about Advantage Media Group's commitment to being a responsible steward of the environment, please visit **www.advantagefamily.com/green**

Inspirational Goaling is available in bulk quantities at special discounts for corporate, institutional, and educational purposes. To learn more about the special programs Advantage Media Group offers, please visit **www.KaizenUniversity.com** or call 1.866.775.1696.

Advantage Media Group is a leading publisher of business, motivation, and self-help authors. Do you have a manuscript or book idea that you would like to have considered for publication? Please visit **www.amgbook.com**

www.ingramcontent.com/pod-product-compliance
Lightning Source LLC
LaVergne TN
LVHW050638100826
845148LV00011B/1901